Who the Hell is Erwin Panofsky?

Who the Hell is Erwin Panofsky?

And what are his theories all about?

Alice Bowden

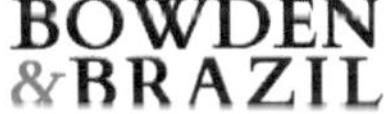

First published in Great Britain in 2019 by
Bowden & Brazil Ltd
Felixstowe, Suffolk, UK.

Second edition 2021

British Library Cataloguing-in-Publication Data
A CIP record for this book is available from The British Library.

Series editor & academic advisor: Dr Joan Hart, Berkeley, California.

ISBN 978-1-9999492-0-4

To find out more about other books and authors in this series, visit www.whothehellis.co.uk

Contents

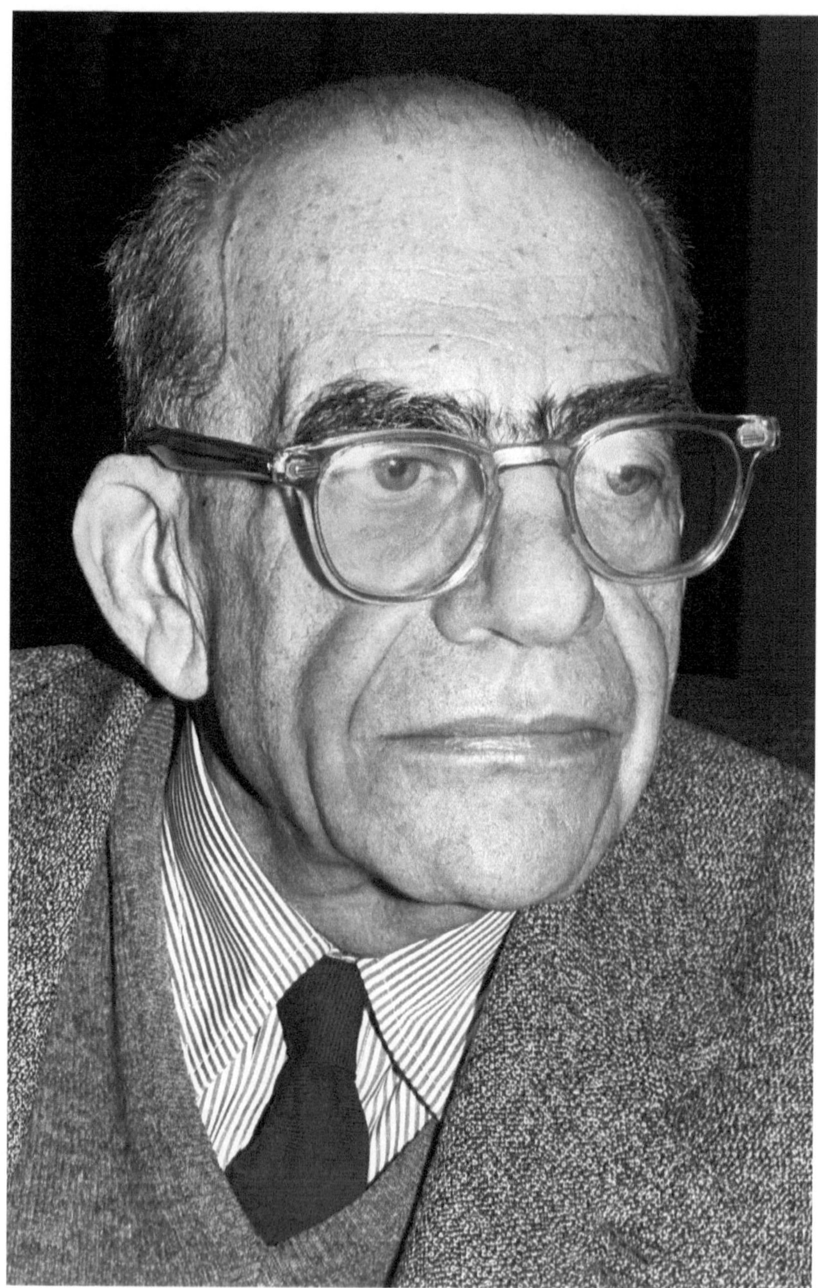

Fig. 1 Erwin Panofsky (1892–1968)

Introduction

When studying any subject, the easiest way to understand its underlying principles is to learn the history of those ideas and the people who formulated them. What was happening in the world at the point that these ideas began to circulate? Which thinkers, in which countries, began to influence each other in such a way that a radical new way of thinking came about? This is what we set out to address in this book.

When Erwin Panofsky began studying art history in 1910, he found himself alongside other radical thinkers and art historians such as Alois Riegl, Heinrich Wolfflin and Aby Warburg. At this time art history was still relatively young as a field of study and, like everything in its infancy, it was going through a bit of a crisis with scholars arguing about whose method was the most efficient. This was Panofsky's starting point, and so it is for this reason that we start the book by looking at Panofsky's background and the ideas that were circulating as he began to think about art and how it might be explored and evaluated. By first exploring and clarifying the ideas of other key historians, it becomes easier both to understand the trajectory of Panofsky's thinking and to see quite how revolutionary his ideas were at the time.

Who the Hell is Erwin Panofsky? looks at Panofsky the person but also a defining moment in art history, where one man brought together several existing approaches to evaluating art and added some powerful new ones of his own. His work is a landmark in the development of the discipline of art history, and so it is critical to understand his ideas if we are to study art history at all. However, while his ideas are brilliant and illuminating, his own writing is not readily accessible, so one of the aims of this book is to decipher his ideas and present them in such a way that they are easy to understand.

Panofsky himself was a humanist and brought a far-reaching approach to the discipline of art history in his endeavour to connect the visual arts with all other areas of culture. He believed that by looking at cultural history alongside art history, an essential 'idea' – a fundamental way that people think collectively – would emerge, creating a unified picture of a historical period. It is this revealing of a people's root cultural principles that makes Panofsky's work so interesting, not only to art historians but also to those studying philosophy, music, semiotics, and the history of science, to name but a few. In short he encourages us to seek a connection between how a person/people/nation thinks and the things that they create. Far from being outdated theories that have been superseded by more modern ones, Panofsky's ideas continue to generate huge interest and cause fervent discussion today.

1. Panofsky's Life Story

Erwin Panofsky was born in Hannover, Germany, on 30 March 1892, to Arnold Panofsky and Caecilie Solling, a wealthy Jewish couple. Arnold Panofsky's family had originally made their fortune from silver mining in Silesia while Arnold went on to work in banking, describing himself as a 'rentier', a man of wealth and leisure. At the time of Panofsky's birth, Germany's economy was booming. It had become one of the major economic powers of Europe and was dominant in the world's chemical industry as well as the coal and steel industries.

Germany was predominantly run by aristocrats, with Kaiser Wilhelm II ruling at that time. But there were also the bourgeoisie who, like Panofsky's family, had grown rich from the success of Germany's industrialization and manufacturing, which continued to grow at a fast rate. Then there was the working class, which grew steadily alongside the German economy. Germany had become a magnet for people leaving their own countries to escape from poverty in search of a better life. Poles and Russians in particular headed in droves, making up a large part of the German work force. What this meant, however, was that there were huge social divisions, with the labourers living in unsatisfactory conditions only a few miles away from the aristocrats' luxurious palaces.

A Gifted Student

For Panofsky though, life was good. After a long history of persecution, German Jews were experiencing legal equality and, thanks to his parents' successful business, Panofsky grew up in Berlin in comfortable surroundings, with good educational opportunities and plenty of financial support. He flourished at his school – the Joachimsthalsche Gymnasium – which had been opened by Emperor Wilhelm I with great fanfare in 1880, when it moved from the suburbs of Berlin to luxurious new buildings in the centre of the city. At this school for gifted children, Panofsky was taught by first-class scholars, including Gino Ravaili, an unconventional teacher who had Panofsky reciting Dante's *Divine Comedy* by heart and speaking fluent Italian by the young age of 16.

Panofsky was a highly intelligent and gifted student, who went on to study philosophy, philology and art history at Berlin University from 1910 to 1914. It was during this period that he won the prestigious Hermann-Grimm Prize for his study of mathematics in the work of German Renaissance painter, Albrecht Dürer (1471–1528). Following that, he matriculated at the universities of Munich and Freiburg, completing his doctorate at Freiberg at the age of just 22, under the guidance of Wilhelm Vöge (1868–1952), one of the most important medievalist art historians of the 20th century. His dissertation, *Dürers Kunsttheorie: vornehmlich in ihrem Verhaltnis zur Kunsttheorie der Italiener* on Dürer's art theory in relation to Italian art theory, was published the following year in Berlin under the title *Die Theoretische Kunstlehre Albrecht Dürers*. With the financial support of his family, Panofsky was able to continue studying art history in Berlin after his doctorate.

A Good Match

In 1916, he married Dorothea 'Dora' Mosse (1885–1965), seven years his senior and also an art historian from a wealthy family. For four centuries, the Mosses had been prominent members of German high culture. Dora's father, Albert Mosse, was a state-court judge in Berlin, and keen for his daughters to receive a university education, which prior to 1908 hadn't been an option. With her father's support and encouragement, Dora and her sister Martha studied French, Latin and Greek in order to get into university, in which they were successful. Dora met Panofsky during her time at university, in one of Adolph Goldschmidt's seminars in Berlin.

Dora and 'Pan', as Panofsky was known to his friends, were clearly intellectually compatible with their shared ideas and passions for Bach concertos, the writings of the Romantic novelist Jean Paul (1763–1825) and the ideas behind German aesthetics, which are revealed in letters that they wrote to one another early on in their relationship. Their union would be long-lasting and certainly advantageous for Panofsky in that Dora proved herself to be one of Panofsky's harshest yet also most perceptive and stimulating critics. She was fairly unconventional and rather ahead of her times, preferring to wear her hair short and accompanying it with suits, ties and wingtip shoes.

When the couple had children, Dora rejected her role as solely mother and housewife and hired a housekeeper so that she might continue with her research and writing. But as it was to be a long time before women were to gain equal opportunities, she struggled to continue her career and fell into the shadow of her husband's success. The Panofskys had two sons, Hans (1917–1988) and Wolfgang (1919–2007), both of whom became professors at American universities: Hans in atmospheric sciences and Wolfgang in Physics.

Starting a Career

Supported by his family's fortune, Panofsky had planned a career as a freelance scholar, devoting himself to art historical research. However, his financial situation was about to change for the worse. After the First World War (from which Panofsky was exempted due to a horse-riding accident), the German Mark decreased significantly in value, resulting in the loss of his family's fortune and in the need for Panofsky to start earning his living. In 1921, he was offered the position of *Privatdozent* (outside lecturer) in Art History at the newly established University of Hamburg, qualifying as a full professor six years later. In Hamburg, Panofsky was amongst scholars such as Edgar Wind (1900–1971) , Hans Liebeschütz (1893–1978), Charles de Tolnay (1899–1981), and perhaps most importantly, Ernst Cassirer (1874–1945). During this time, and alongside Cassirer, he also spent a lot of time at the Warburg Institute and with its members, Rudolf Wittkower (1901–1971), Fritz Saxl (1890–1948), Gertrud Bing (1892–1964), and Aby Warburg (1866–1929) himself. Together they wrote a series of lectures over a number of years published as the *Vorträge der Bibliothek Warburg*. This was to prove an important association of brilliant minds that would almost certainly have shaped Panofsky's ideas and the path that his theories were to take, as we shall see in Chapter 2.

With a thick moustache, reminiscent of Nietzsche, covering his top lip, long whiskers hanging down over his ears, and longish hair with a receding hairline, Panofsky had a rather romantic appearance. He was extremely popular both amongst his peers and particularly amongst his students, attracting a full audience to his lectures. His talks were heartfelt, convincing and fluent in nature, his ideas traditional yet innovative and progressive. He had a tendency to introduce the obscure and was notorious for suggesting that his students read books not included in the curriculum as background reading for their humanistic studies, stating, 'Gentlemen, you have yet to discover the value of useless knowledge' (Heckscher, 1969). He often continued debates and discussions with students after lectures back at his apartment long into the night. According to his friend and fellow art historian, William S. Heckscher (1904–1999), he had an incredible brain that could retain both visual and verbal information, enabling him to create whole chapters of as-yet un-written books in his head, and then, without having written down a single word, recite the chapter verbatim at a later date. Panofsky's lectures in Hamburg had found an ideal setting; nestled between the Warburg library and the art gallery in a conservatively artistic city, this art historical centre became the recipient of international intellectual progressive ideas. Panofsky became known for his humanistic approach towards art history with the aim of changing it from an antiquarian discipline to one that embraced neighbouring fields, while at the same time safeguarding traditional methods.

New York

During the period of 1931 to 1934, Panofsky took on the role of Visiting Professor of Fine Arts at New York University, which obliged him to 'commute', sharing his time between the two universities on an alternate term basis. This dual role proved to be fortuitous for two reasons. Firstly, in that he found himself in a country where the discipline of art history was far less inhibited by the ethnocentricity and traditionalism of European art historians. Panofsky's ideas were received enthusiastically and he was held in high esteem by colleagues and students alike. In 1933 he wrote the article 'Classical Mythology in Medieval Art' in collaboration with his associate Fritz Saxl, which essentially gained him recognition within American humanistic scholarship. But Panofsky's advent into the world of American art history was also to prove fortunate for another reason. It was at this time that war was looming on the horizon in Europe. Following the appointment of Adolf Hitler as Chancellor of Germany on 30 January 1933, the persecution of the Jews began again in full force. A Nazi boycott of Jewish businesses began on 1 April in the beginning of an anti-Semitic campaign, which was to grow to terrifying proportions.

Universities in particular were targeted, the 'Jewish question' having been raised and made a primary issue by the leading student organization, *Deutschen Hochschulring*, back in 1921. It was, after all, the German universities that were educating the future leaders of the Third Reich. According to Rubenstein and Roth in their study of the Holocaust, 'Two-thirds of the Security Police and SD leadership had university degrees and one-third had earned doctorates, very largely in law, and had been active in one or more völkisch or ultranationalistic groups as students' (2003). Thus, it must not have come as much of a surprise to Panofsky when, in April 1933, he was dismissed from his position at Hamburg University when the new Nazi Law for the Restoration of the Professional Civil Service came into effect, which meant that Jews were no longer able to work in government positions.

Moving to America

With his whole future in academia threatened, Panofsky returned briefly to Germany in the summer of 1933 to supervise some of his students who were at the final stages of their dissertations, before moving permanently to the USA in 1934. Although Panofsky was lucky in that he managed to escape the atrocities taking place in Germany and save his immediate family by moving them first to Britain and then later to America in 1934, he lost around 35 relatives who were unable to escape and who were subsequently placed in concentration camps. Panofsky's ties with New York University made it easier for him to move to America than for others in the same position. Upon his arrival he continued to teach at NYU and also at Princeton University. A year later, he was offered a position as a professor at the Institute for Advanced Studies in Princeton, where he remained until his retirement in 1963. The move to America also proved advantageous to Dora who finally found herself accepted by the 'gentlemen scholars' of the university and was able to resume her career as an art historian, despite America not being much more ahead in terms of equality between the sexes. Having lived in her husband's shadow for many years, Dora, at the age of 58, finally proved herself as a scholar and went on to write articles and books.

Needless to say, Panofsky's time at Princeton was incredibly productive. Surrounded by colleagues who were also close friends and working in surroundings which enticed visiting scholars from all around the world, Panofsky was in his element. In 1939, he published one of his most acclaimed works, *Studies in Iconology*. According to Heckscher, it was this book that 'marks the turning point at which iconology ceased to be an ancillary

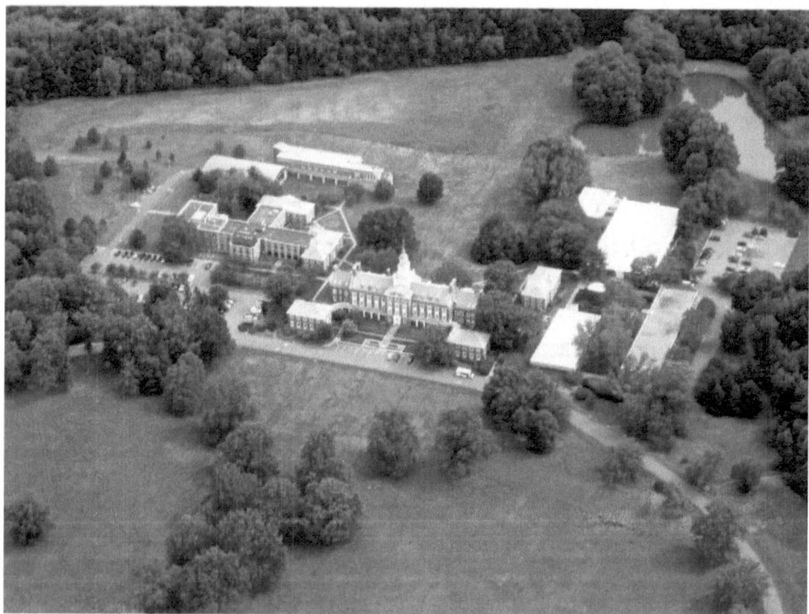

Fig. 2 Institute for Advanced Studies, Princeton, New Jersey, USA.

discipline and became an indispensable part of art historical method' (1969). Following this came a succession of published works: *The Life and Art of Albrecht Dürer* (1943), which brought together much of his research over the years on the artist; following that Panofsky wrote *Abbot Suger on the Abbey Church of St.-Denis* (1946), *Gothic Architecture and Scholasticism* (1951) and *Early Netherlandish Painting* (1953), which was the product of his Charles Eliot Norton lectures at Harvard during the period of 1947–48 (it was the American custom to put lectures together in such a way that they could be published at a later date – and this certainly suited Panofsky's method of working). In this two-volume monograph of northern Renaissance art, Panofsky makes a convincing iconographical study of how even the most visually realistic works of this period embody complex Christian symbolism. One such revelation was the uncovering of Jan van Eyck's *Arnolfini Portrait* (1434) as a pictorial marriage certificate.

More books followed during the 1950s, two of which Panofsky co-wrote (in equal contribution) with his wife, Dora. These joint projects were *Pandora's Box: The Changing Aspects of a Mythical Symbol* (1956) and *The Iconography of the Galerie François Ier at Fontainebleau* (1958). *Pandora's Box* prompted the nickname 'PanDora' for the Panofskys, combining the pet names that they were known by, much to the amusement of the critics and the resignation of the Panofskys themselves.

At the end of 1959, owing to the postponement of his retirement, Panofsky received a somewhat premature commemoration for his work at the Institute. In his own commemoration of Panofsky in 1969, Heckscher describes Panofsky's embarrassment at being present at a ceremony for the remembrance of his own life, when he was still very much alive and involved in the institute and his work there. One of the final books Panofsky wrote while at Princeton was *Renaissance and Renascences in Western Art* (1960), again resulting from his lectures – this time the Gottesman lectures that he presented at Uppsala University in Sweden. Panofsky puts forward that before the Italian Renaissance, smaller classical renaissances can be detected in both art and literature periodically throughout the medieval period – a conception that is taken for granted today.

Retirement and Death

Panofsky finally retired from Princeton in 1963, although it wasn't retirement proper as he was immediately appointed as the Professor of Fine Arts at New York University, and he continued to publish works. His strong belief in the humanist tradition remained and is evident in the many articles he wrote during his last decade when he was apt to explore further afield, as the often bizarre titles suggest: 'Canopus Deus, the Iconography of a Non-Existent God' (1961); 'Homage to Fracastoro' (a study of the role that syphilis played in Renaissance art) (1961); 'The Ideological Antecedents of the Rolls-Royce Radiator' (1963); and 'The Mouse that Michelangelo Failed to Carve' (1964), are some of the more ambiguous, alongside his more traditional writings, such as *Tomb Sculpture* (1964) and *Saturn and Melancholy* (1964).

In 1965, Panofsky's wife, Dora, died from a protracted illness and, not long after, Panofsky married Gerda Soergel, an art historian almost four decades his junior. His friend and colleague Heckscher describes Panofsky, in the two years that followed, as having a new lease of energy, travelling abroad and rediscovering a youthful enthusiasm for life after caring for his invalid wife for so long. He even ended a 33-year absence from his mother country and made a trip back to Germany where he was awarded an order of merit from West Germany – the *Pour le Mérite* – as recognition of extraordinary personal achievement. Despite this honour and his pride at being part of the tradition of German art historical scholarship, Panofsky gave his lecture in English, an affirmation perhaps of his claim to being 'free from what may be suspected as retroactive German patriotism' (1955a).

Panofsky died in 1968, after a series of heart attacks. On his deathbed he wrote a poem in Latin, which speaks of his love of life mingled with the bitterness of old age and which is a testament to a mind as sharp and creative at the end of his life as it had been at the beginning:

> *'Dulcia sane et amara simul praebere senectus*
> *Cernitur, atque mihi munus utrumque placet.*
> *Pallescunt frondes; stellae tamen usque manebunt.*
> *Lucet, non urit Sole cadente Venus.'* (Heckscher, 1969)

> *[Indeed, old age appears to offer sweet and bitter things*
> *simultaneously, and either gift delights me.*
> *Leaves lose their colour, and yet the stars remain.*
> *The sun sets and Venus shines, but does not burn.]*

Erwin Panofsky's Timeline

Erwin Panofsky

- **1892** Born in Hannover, Germany
- **1910-14** Studied philosophy, philology and art history at Berlin University
- **1916** Marries Dorothea 'Dora' Mosse
- **1917** Birth of son, Hans
- **1919** Birth of son, Wolfgang
- **1921** Takes up position as *Privatdozent* at University of Hamburg
- **1931-34** Appointed Visiting Professor of Fine Arts at New York University
- **1933** Dismissed from Hamburg University
- **1934** Moves to America
- **1935** Appointed professor at the Institute for Advanced Studies in Princeton
- **1939** Publishes ***Studies in Iconology***

World Events

- **1904** International Woman Suffrage Alliance founded in Berlin
- **1905** Russian Revolution
- **1914** Beginning of WWI
- **1918** WWI ends; Spanish flu pandemic
- **1919** Prohibition in America
- **1920-21** Russian famine, 5 million die
- **1923** Economic crisis in Weimar Republic in Germany
- **1929** Black Tuesday leads to Great Depression in America
- **1933** Adolf Hitler appointed Chancellor of Germany; Nazi boycott of Jewish businesses begins
- **1936** Hitler pulls Germany out of the League of Nations
- **1938** *Kristallnacht* carried out by Nazis
- **1939** WWII breaks out

1943 Publishes ***The Life and Art of Albrecht Dürer***

1946 Publishes ***Abbot Suger on the Abbey Church of St.-Denis***

1951 Publishes ***Gothic Architecture and Scholasticism***

1953 Publishes ***Early Netherlandish Painting***

1956 Publishes ***Pandora's Box: The Changing Aspects of a Mythical Symbol***, co-written with Dora

1958 Publishes ***The Iconography of the Galerie François Ier at Fontainebleau***, co-written with Dora

1960 Publishes ***Renaissance and Renascences in Western Art***

1963 Retires from Princeton; appointed Professor of Fine Arts at New York University

1964 Publishes ***Tomb Sculpture*** and ***Saturn and Melancholy***

1965 Dora dies

1966 Marries Gerda Soergel, an art historian four decades his junior

1968 Panofsky dies after a series of heart attacks

1945 End of WWII; Nuremberg trials begin

1949 NATO is established

1950-53 Korean War

1955 Beginning of the Vietnam War

1956 Suez Crisis

1957 Soviet Union launches Sputnik 1 into orbit

1961 Berlin Wall is constructed

1962 Cuban Missile Crisis

1963 President John F. Kennedy is assassinated

1964 America outlaws racial segregation in schools; Civil Rights Act is signed

1966 Emergence of the Black Power movement in America

1968 Student and worker uprisings in France

2. Influences on Panofsky's Thinking

The scholars that Panofsky came across during his time in Berlin, Munich and Freiberg were to have a huge influence on the way his ideas developed. In the academic world of history in the mid-to-late 19th century, there were two different approaches towards what constituted a valid working method: there were those who followed the more traditional antiquarian method, which had a distinctive positivist angle to it, and those that were neo-Hegelians (following the ideas of the philosopher Georg Hegel (1770–1831)) which took on a much more idealist approach. We will look at these two approaches shortly. However, historians that specialized in the field of art were often a little more creative in their approach than their contemporaries in the field of history, and they tended to waver between the two camps, picking and choosing elements that they considered to be the answer to finding a comprehensive art historical method.

Antiquarians

The antiquarians believed that history should follow the methodology of the physical sciences and should therefore be based upon first-hand factual evidence such as diaries, letters, government documents, diplomatic reports and eyewitness accounts. In the same way that the physical world operates according to general laws, like gravity, those art historians that leaned towards a positivist method believed that the study of art should encompass a basic procedure of observation, reflection and verification as established by a scientific method. They avoided theory or any kind of moral judgement, aiming to present nothing but pure fact.

Neo-Hegelians

The neo-Hegelians also set out to turn history into a natural science, except their method was based on theory rather than fact. They were much more interested in metaphysics – the branch of philosophy that deals with abstract concepts such as being, knowing, time and space. They believed that through a study of the particularities of history, it was possible to uncover generalized principles at work (like a sort of 'motor' that controls events) – something that is known as 'historical determinism'.

The Formalist Method

So while the antiquarians were dealing with excavations of archival material, the idealists were using imaginative insight. At this time, the study of art was almost solely based on a formalist method. That is, historians looked for answers by analyzing the purely visual aspects of a work like form, style and composition. Any contextual aspect, such as the historical and social background behind the work, the life of the artist or even the iconography (the interpretation of visual images or symbols) was considered to be merely supporting material. It wasn't until the 20th century that art historians with a structuralist stance (interpreting and analyzing human behaviour, culture and experience) began arguing against studying art from a purely visual viewpoint.

A New Way of Seeing

While at university, Panofsky was taught by several art historians who were formalists in their approach and who would have introduced him to both the antiquarian and metaphysical methods of studying art history. In Freiberg, he met Wilhelm Vöge, under whom he wrote his dissertation. Vöge specialized in medieval art and was the founder of modern stylistic analysis, which looks at the relationship between works of art by comparing universally accepted characteristics. This was a much more in-depth stylistic analysis than those that preceded it. Each work in turn would be subjected to extensive research into every individual characteristic, giving the historian an insight into the art period as a whole. This meant that rather than simply analyzing the form and material of an artwork, Vöge would also delve into other fields, such as iconography, psychology and even paleography (the study of ancient writing) in order to find a historical and contextual background for the different elements of an artwork. His way of working meant that he would waver between the method of the antiquarians and that of the neo-Hegelians. By doing so he uncovered a multitude of detail in a very scientific way but at the same time he offered up valuable insights that were independent from the facts – an approach that is not unlike the one that Panofsky would later adopt.

A little later, back in Berlin, Panofsky attended lectures by Adolph Goldschmidt (1863–1944), who was to supervise Panofsky's post-doctoral work. Like Vöge, Goldschmidt employed a formalist methodology that included iconography and was incredibly analytical and precise in its approach. However, whereas Vöge would analyse an artwork using feeling and sensibility, Goldschmidt was more of a positivist and would never offer up observations that weren't based upon facts and evidence. What will become apparent as we go on to look at Panofsky's own ideas is how he takes certain analytical elements from his former tutors and builds upon them to create his own humanistic methodology.

During his time at university Panofsky studied the theories and methods of two of the most influential art historians of the time: Alois Riegl (1858–1905) and Heinrich Wölfflin (1864–1945).

Heinrich Wölfflin

Wölfflin, along with many of his contemporaries, set out to find a method that had the same precision and attention to detail as that of the natural sciences. But at the same time he believed that it was vital that an art historical method be based upon more than just collating the facts. What he was committed to finding was a general principle or law that would enable him to interpret the facts. By way of a solution Wölfflin came up with his 'principles of art history', which he published in 1915. Being essentially a formalist, Wölfflin wanted to explain the changes that occur in style over time. While he believed in historical determinism (see above), he didn't believe that it was possible to identify patterns of development through looking at an artwork within its social context alone. He felt that it was much more relevant to target the specifically visual characteristics of an artwork, such as its structural and compositional features, in order to reveal the way style develops historically.

Wölfflin was the first to introduce the practice of using two image projectors (back then they were called magic lanterns) in lectures in order to compare two works of art. He believed that the style of any epoch could be attributed to one of two different ways of formal construction. He called these the 'classic' and the 'baroque'. By showing the contrasting styles of two paintings from two different periods he set out to prove that the visual characteristics of a work of art have their own 'laws' of development. He based his analysis on five pairs of contrasting principles:

1. linear vs. painterly (clearly distinguished form vs. forms merging)
2. plane vs. recession (flat surfaces vs. depth and perspective)
3. closed vs. open form (strict and self-contained vs. irregularity and movement)
4. multiplicity vs. unity (independently functioning parts vs. parts that are only meaningful in the context of a whole)
5. clarity vs. lacking definition (comprehensible, exact form vs. unclear forms that hint at clarity)

His aim was to show that the first in the pairs of concepts (linear, plane etc.), which he classed as 'classic' must always come

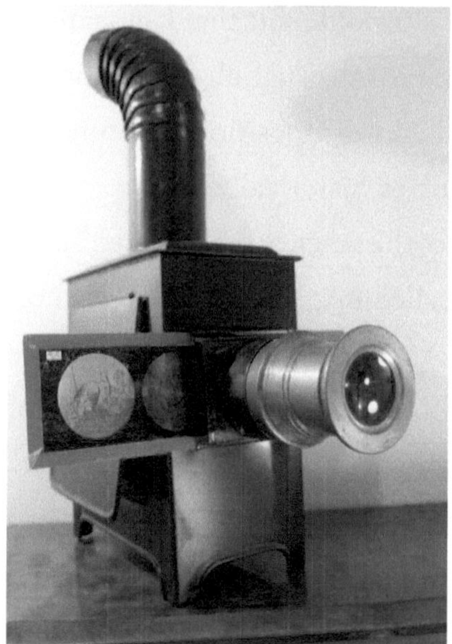

Fig. 3 A 19th-century magic lantern, as would have been used by Wölfflin.

first before it can develop into the second of the pairs of concepts (painterly, recession etc.) which he referred to as 'baroque'. So for example, Wölfflin put forth that it is necessary for an artist to learn the skill of painting with clarity before it is possible to develop a style of working that lacks definition. He believed that vision has its own history, separate from the social or cultural history of an artwork; that human beings actually see the world differently in different periods of history.

The same year that Wölfflin published Principles of Art History (1915), Panofsky wrote an essay, titled 'Das Problem des Stils in der bildenden Kunst' (The Problem of Style in the Visual Arts), challenging Wölfflin's highly regarded work. The essay shows Panofsky engaging with current ideas of well-respected mentors with the aim of developing his own concepts in order to bring something new to the field of art history. His criticism of Wölfflin's method shows us that he already believed that it is essential for an artwork to be analyzed both visually and historically. In his essay, he takes up Wölfflin's assertion that each period has a different way of seeing. He argues that it is not seeing that changes in history, but the interpretation of what we see that changes. Every person possesses an aesthetic choice and it is this that changes as we choose to express our ideas about the visual world in different ways. For Panofsky, a study of the purely visual aspects of an artwork, distinct from the artist him or herself and their cultural and social surroundings, just wasn't tenable. But he clearly saw great value in Wölfflin's method of using contrasting pairs of concepts, as he would later go on to form his own, which we will look at in more detail in Chapter 3.

Alois Riegl

Five years later, Panofsky tackled Riegl in his essay, '*Der Begriff des Kunstwollens*' (The Concept of Kunstwollens, 1920). There is no direct translation for 'kunstwollen', but it has been interpreted variously as 'that which wills art' or 'artistic volition', and refers to the force driving the development of style, implying that the evolution of artistic form is autonomous. This force is a synthesis of the whole artistic phenomena: the art from a period, a people, a country/region, as well as the individual artist.

Essentially Panofsky was in favour of Riegl's kunstwollen as it was based on social psychology, that is, an artist's social interactions, their origins and those effects on the individual artist. But, as with Wölfflin, he still believed that the method didn't go far enough. For Panofsky, if the kunstwollen was a combination of everything connected to an artwork then it must, in theory, include the very nature of an artwork itself: its intrinsic value. Therefore, art historical methods that examine an artwork in relation to something else, for example, how cultural

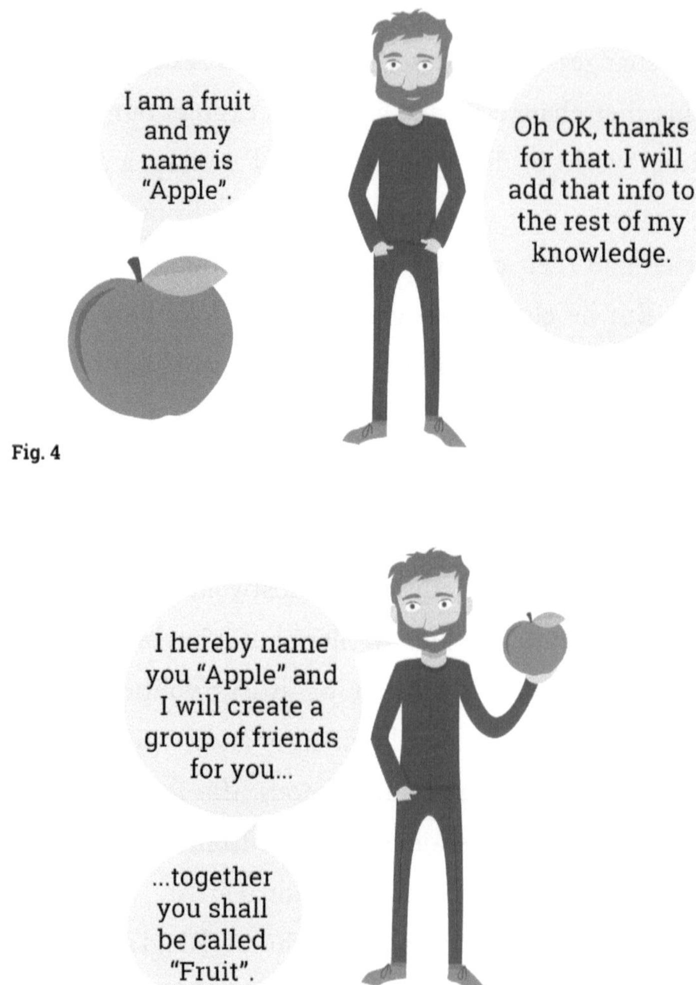

Fig. 4

Fig. 5

conditions affect an artwork, and how an artwork develops through history, must also look at an artwork separately – at its own being – in order to really get to the bottom of the fundamentals of art history. It is this that Panofsky suggests Riegl hadn't accomplished and what he, Panofsky, aimed to find: a third way of looking at an artistic object. He referred to this as an 'Archimedean viewpoint' – a hypothetical viewpoint from which one can observe a subject objectively. This, he hoped, would provide his formal and cultural method with the philosophical interpretation needed to make it comprehensive.

Cassirer

During his time at the University of Hamburg Panofsky met many clever and inspiring scholars. One colleague in particular, Ernst Cassirer, so impressed him that he attended Cassirer's lectures alongside the students. It was at this time that Panofsky began to see how he might develop Riegl's concept of kunstwollen in order to find his Archimedean viewpoint.

In an essay written in 1924 for the Warburg library, '*Die Perspektive als "symbolische Form."*' (Perspective as symbolic form), Panofsky shows an affiliation with Cassirer's theories. The title itself relates directly to Cassirer's most renowned work, *The Philosophy of Symbolic Forms* (1923–1929), in which Cassirer sets out to show that we do not gain knowledge about the objects around us from the actual object itself (Fig. 4), but instead it is our human reasoning and imagination that creates our knowledge of that object (Fig. 5).

Cassirer interpreted the ways in which we express ourselves, which shape how we think and what we think, as 'symbolic forms', and it was these symbolic forms in all their diversity that preoccupied him for most of his working life. He believed that all parts of culture – language, science, myth, art, religion – all work together to transform our impressions of the world into manifestations of our human spirit. In other words, in every part of culture we take in what we see or experience and then outwardly turn it into something concrete, something that reflects our inner self. Therefore our 'nature' is embodied in our 'work'. Cassirer concludes that the upshot of this is that reality itself cannot be understood with any real validity: it is always tainted by our reasoning and our imagination.

When looking at artworks from a philosophical point of view, Cassirer (influenced by Kant) sees a work of art as having a sort of intention without an actual purpose. So, unlike, say, a bowl, whose 'intention' is to be round and concave so that it can hold food or liquid (its 'purpose'), an artwork has an 'intention' to be produced using marble/canvas/paint etc., but with no purpose other than being as it is. However, despite seeing an artwork as an autonomous and isolated object, Cassirer theorizes that it must also be subject to cause and effect. He explains this apparent inconsistency by using the example of how there is no contradiction between the beauty of nature and the laws of nature – they are two separate things that are mutually dependent on one another (think, chicken and egg – which came first?). Causality is about understanding the development over time whereas seeing an object as self-contained is a matter of appreciating its structure. It is the marriage between autonomy and causality that particularly interests Cassirer.

In his essay on perspective, Panofsky begins by looking at this geometrical practice in the same way that Cassirer looked at forms of expression. He sees perspective as a symbolic form in the way that it is a humanly constructed rule that cannot be objective as it is based on the way a person sees the world. His argument

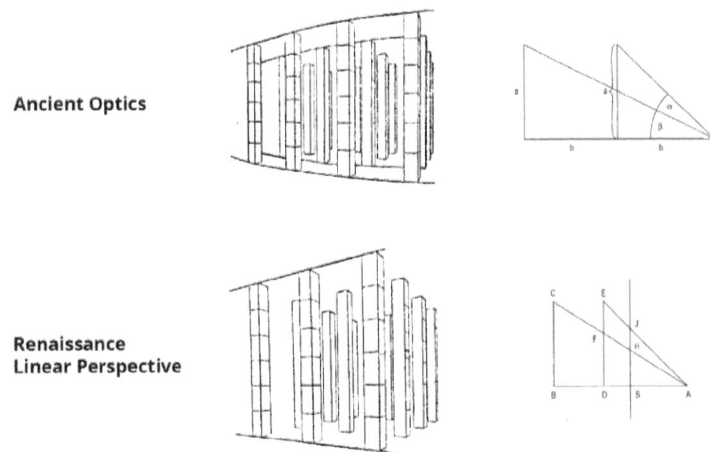

Fig. 6 Differing rules of perspective

is based on two main notions: first, we do not see with a single, motionless eye; and second, that the plane section through the cone of sight is not proven to be identical to that visual image that we actually see. Our 'retinal image' shows shapes of objects projected onto a concave surface, whereas a 'visual image' goes by the notion that the shape of the object is projected onto a plane. Panofsky argues that the rules of perspective have changed over time, with each era thinking differently.

Ancient optics differed from Renaissance perspective, in that they comprehended the field of vision as a sphere, and therefore maintained that the projections of objects onto that sphere are determined by angles. Whereas during the Renaissance period, linear perspectival construction was used, whereby they believed that a straight line is seen as straight despite the fact that the eye projects onto a sphere and not a plane. They therefore made their calculations based on distance, rather than on angles.

Any Renaissance teachings or translations of Euclid – a Greek mathematician of around 300 BCE, whose teachings ancient optics were based upon – either completely left out Euclid's Eighth Theorem or changed it so that its original meaning was lost.

Ever since, we have accepted the geometrical construction of Renaissance paintings as being the correct way of 'seeing'. Therefore, Panofsky argues, perspective can be seen as a 'mythical structure' – a system that has been created in order to structure our visible world so that we can make sense of it. In his essay, Panofsky refers directly to Cassirer and his 'symbolic forms', and the way they transform our impressions of the world in order to argue that perspective is a symbolic form. He believes that the specific spatial system used in a particular age shares common principles with other symbolic forms of that age, such as those that can be found in their philosophical and scientific texts.In the following chapter we will look at how Panofsky develops his ideas from those that he has taken from Wölfflin, Riegl and Cassirer.

Cultural Influences

As well as being influenced directly by people that he came into contact with, Panofsky would have absorbed something of the ideas and theories that were popular within his cultural milieu at that time. This would have included cultural history, philosophical thinking (as we saw with Cassirer), semiotics – the study of sign systems – and linguistics. There is evidence of this in his iconological methodology. In *Studies in Iconology*, Panofsky begins with the example of a man lifting his hat in greeting in order to explain how we use signs to convey meaning. The ideas that Panofsky discusses in his book (which we will look at in more detail in Chapter 4) echo the studies of the Swiss linguist and semiotician, Ferdinand de Saussure (1857–1913) in his book *Course in General Linguistics* (1959). Saussure was interested in the way that the rules of our language system, and the way that we put them into practice, contribute to and depend upon the meanings of our current time and place. He therefore shared the belief with Panofsky that the way we express ourselves can best be interpreted in its contemporary cultural and social context. Iconology, in the same way as semiotics, set out to prove that acts of communication – be it visual or linguistic – develop both consciously and unconsciously in the history of mankind.

Panofsky's interest in the historical content of a work of art was regarded at the time as being the domain of the cultural historian rather than the art historian. But by now it should be clear that Panofsky was prone to crossing boundaries. He regarded the visual arts as being part of a creative whole that included philosophy, religion, science and literature – a trait of his humanist approach. There were many cultural historians of the 19th century who also believed in combining cultural disciplines and it is with them that we can identify the foundations of Panofsky's intellectual formation.

Three cultural theorists/historians in particular were to have a fundamental influence on Panofsky's ideas. Georg Hegel (1770–1831), Jacob Burckhardt (1818–1897) and Wilhelm Dilthey (1833–1911) all put forth a contextualist critique of formalism, arguing that the visual arts cannot be understood purely from a study of its form and style but must be seen in terms of being part of a universe of culture.

Georg Hegel

Georg Hegel was one of the most influential historians and philosophers of his time. He is perhaps best known for his dialectical method, whereby he believed that history had its own rational, systematic mode of working that consisted of three stages of development. The first, the 'thesis', reaches a point in its existence where it begins to cause a reaction. This creates the second stage, the 'antithesis', which contradicts the thesis and in so doing creates a tension. This is resolved by the third stage, the 'synthesis'. So, for example, Hegel sees one era as encompassing an 'idea' of the world – a 'World Spirit' – which then comes up against conflict which results in its destruction and the consequent birth of a new world view. Hegel believed that history must always pass through a negative stage in order to evolve.

In the 1820s, Hegel gave a series of lectures on aesthetics, and a collection of these were published in 1835. These had a marked effect on art historical study, influencing art historians no matter what their theoretical approach. Although Panofsky rejected Hegel's idealist hypotheses, as described at the beginning of this chapter, his method followed Hegel's philosophy of history and the need to bring form and context together. As early as 1930, in an article that he wrote as a study for the Warburg Library, Panofsky shows his belief that a work of art is more than just aesthetic form and must benefit from a study of its historical content. From then on, he set about putting the art object back into its historical situation amid its cultural surroundings. In his book, *Gothic Architecture and Scholasticism* (1951), Panofsky shows how the development of both Gothic architecture and scholasticism (the system of theology and philosophy based on early Christianity and the teachings of Aristotle) proceeds in tandem suggesting that periods of history and their cultural phenomena act in unity. This echoes Hegel's thoughts in his Aesthetics that art, alongside philosophy, religion and science, is part of the same world spirit and its history expresses the same fundamental theories that can be seen in the history of its cultural counterparts. Where it differs substantially, however, is that for Hegel, content is seen in terms of world spirit rather than Panofsky's analysis of works of art in terms of their individual historical content. Hegel's approach tends to look at art in a more metaphysical way, looking at the more abstract concept of human creativity rather than the historical problems and qualities that arise from the content of an artwork.

Jacob Burckhardt

Burckhardt's method involved studying individual details of a cultural period, before situating them in their greater context. Although he rejected Hegel's metaphysical world spirit and his three stages of development, he believed in a spirit of a kind that showed a unity of thinking between the arts, society and politics. Burckhardt's method was primarily synchronic, meaning that he focused his study on the aspects of one age, rather than looking at how culture and humanism developed and evolved through time, as Hegel did. It is this approach that Panofsky uses in his own iconological method. In his description of the third part of his analysis (see Chapter 4)), Panofsky explains how it is possible to determine the content of an artwork by 'ascertaining those underlying principles which reveal the basic attitude of a nation, a period, a class, a religious or philosophical persuasion – qualified by one personality and condensed into one work' (1955a). (Note his use of the singular.)

Wilhelm Dilthey

The third cultural historian that had a formative influence on Panofsky was Wilhelm Dilthey. At the beginning of this chapter we looked at the criteria for each of the world views that existed around the time of Burckhardt and Dilthey: Hegelian metaphysical idealism and antiquarian positivism. Dilthey was caught somewhere between the two, striving to find a way to combine the scientific method of excavating the facts, ordering them, and then interpreting them, with the humanist method of applying 'imaginative insight' in order to find relevant connections between facts that will broaden our understanding. He also believed that it was vital to look at an artwork through the eyes of the artist and the period he was from, maintaining a historical distance from the work being studied in order to remain objective.

In a lecture at Princeton in 1938 on 'The History of Art as a Humanistic Discipline', (later published) Panofsky echoes Dilthey's beliefs. He describes the two processes as being 'interconnected', arguing that engaging in archaeological research and using intuition in a creative way should not be separated by prioritizing one over the other. In fact they merge as one, each giving weight to the other. In a footnote to this essay, Panofsky emphasizes the importance of maintaining objectivity, warning that art historians must separate themselves from their own experience of the artwork and recreate the experience of the artist in question. What is obvious is that Panofsky has included two of Dilthey's fundamental precepts in his methodological approach: the need to find an intermediate state between the conflicting approaches of the idealist and the positivist; and the need to maintain an objective distance by looking at a historical period through the eyes of a contemporary.

The Warburg Library

Another art historian whose interests and method veered towards cultural history rather than the more traditional aestheticizing art historical approach was Aby Warburg. A scholar specializing in Renaissance art in an intellectual and social context, Warburg taught at the University of Hamburg, although he never took on a full-time position. Wherever possible, he advocated the ideas and methods of his life's work, which took on the form of a private library and later turned into a research institute. Still in existence today, albeit now located in London, the Warburg Library of Cultural Studies is the result of Warburg's interest in cultural history and his obsessive collecting of books. Panofsky was a huge fan of the library, in all probability because of its unique cross-disciplinary referencing system: instead of being ordered by subject matter, Warburg arranged his books by

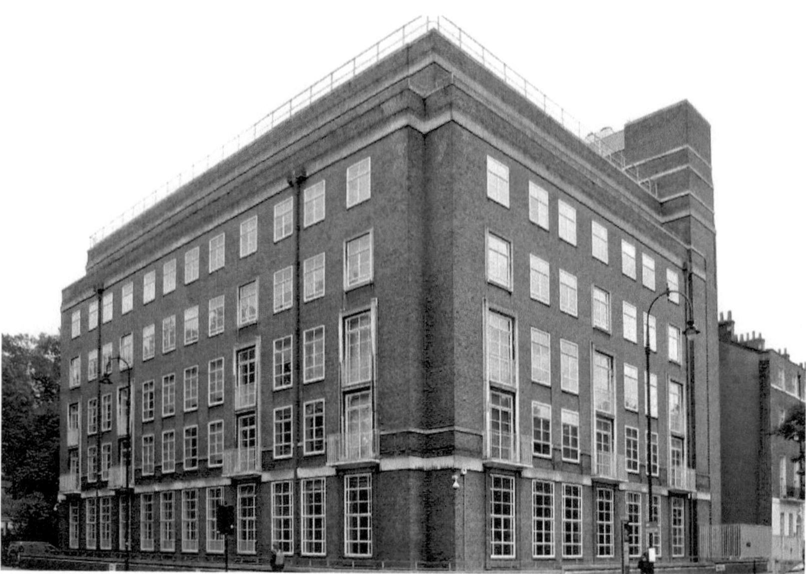

Fig. 7 Warburg Institute, formed in Hamburg, Germany, and later moved to London where it became affiliated with the University of London.

relevance. If he saw a connection between medieval astrology and modern astronomy, then those texts would be placed side by side. Essentially, the library is catalogued by theme and goes by a sort of 'law of the good neighbour', whereby when one searches for a particular book, one will, at the same time, come across another book that is relevant and that opens up doors to other lines of research. For Panofsky, who believed in the relevance of an artwork's cultural surroundings, the contents of the Warburg Library must have been like Aladdin's Cave.

Panofsky first met Warburg in 1912 as a student in Berlin, when he attended Warburg's lecture in Rome on the significance of astrology in the stylistic evolution of Italian painting, which was largely an iconological analysis. Later, teaching at the University of Hamburg and situated close to the Warburg Library, which would later become affiliated to the university, Panofsky became a regular visitor. It was here that Panofsky became part of a research group, which included Ernst Cassirer, Aby Warburg, Fritz Saxl, Rudolf Wittkower and Gertrud Bing, and where they gave lectures and presented their work. They became well known for a series of published lectures known as the *Warburg Vorträge*, as well as a series of monographic studies. Being somewhat of a specialist on Albrecht Dürer, Panofsky was asked to help Saxl, Warburg's assistant, in completing a study of Dürer's *Melencolia I* (1514) (see Chapter 5) that Warburg had started before falling ill. Panofsky and Saxl followed Warburg's method of interpreting the work iconographically so as to produce a monograph that, for the first time, set out to show how Dürer dealt with certain traditions of painting (the use of geometry, the depiction of particular characters etc.) in order to convey a new way of perceiving 'melancholy'.

We can see Warburg's influence on Panofsky's ideas in his work *Hercules am Scheidewege* (Hercules at the Crossroads), which was published by the Warburg Library as one of their monographic studies in 1930. Panofsky follows the history of a theme (here Vice and Virtue) and its evolution to reveal the perspective of the artist, Dürer, and the period in which he lived. This is the first of Panofsky's works that begins to look at iconography as a possible direction for art historical inquiry and is an example of Panofsky's intention to turn an aesthetic-oriented, antiquarian art history into a humanistic discipline, which 'borrowed' from neighbouring fields while at the same time retaining traditional art historical methods.

The War and America

Panofsky's interest in humanism no doubt developed from his being witness to the politicization of the arts by the Nazis. Germany had always been a nation that actively embraced the arts into its society so it is hardly surprising that it became a tool of political and ideological means in order to promote the progressively fascist views of the German nation. It is art's loss of neutrality that likely prompted Panofsky to write his essay 'The History of Art as a Humanistic Discipline' (1940), which reflects his concern with the interference in art and its subsequent loss of autonomy and freedom.

Panofsky's definition of humanism and its nemeses in this essay show where his ideas for finding a more objective art history have developed. For Panofsky, humanism is more to do with attitude than with any sort of ideology. He defines it as the insistence upon rationality and freedom, which results in a need for responsibility; and the acceptance of imperfection and weakness, which results in the need for tolerance. His description of those who rally against humanism is clearly that of his fellow citizens in his contemporary Germany; those that he labels 'determinists', 'authoritarians', 'hero-worshipers', and even 'aestheticists'. Panofsky sees a humanist as being one who is against authority but supports tradition. Ultimately, his belief in a humanistic history of art proved to be his saving grace. Whether it was due to his humanistic method or simply his reputation as an eminent scholar of medieval and northern Renaissance art, his invitation to lecture at New York University not only allowed him an easy exit from Nazi Germany, but would also open many doors for him in his chosen discipline.

Art history, as a subject of study, was essentially born in the German-speaking countries in Europe – Germany, Austria and Switzerland – where it was first acknowledged as an established academic discipline. But on the other side of the Atlantic, the Americans were fast catching up. Having no established tradition, art history in America came about through the coming together of scholars of philosophy, theology, architecture, classical philology and literature. Over the first few decades of the 20th century the discipline expanded at a great rate in the USA and was going through a sort of golden age at the time that Hitler came to power in Germany. For an art historian who believed in an art history that should encompass the study of culture as a whole, rather than the more restricted traditional way of the antiquarians, America must have been an exciting and stimulating place for Panofsky and his peers when they arrived there during the WWII. In an essay written in 1953 on his experience as a relocated European, Panofsky describes the abundance of art historical treasures and the accessibility of pertinent material to all. The countless exhibitions, illuminating lectures and funded research projects available created a 'spirit of discovery and experimentation' (1955a) that Panofsky hadn't been privy to before.

Another advantage that Panofsky found in the New World was America's sense of objectivity. Whereas in Europe art historians tended to think of art with reference to national and regional boundaries and bias, in America, seen from a distance, there were no such restrictions. The boundaries could be determined objectively as there was no personal or established prejudice. Historical distance was achieved through America's cultural and geographical distance. For Panofsky this was essential for the art historical method that he was striving to put in place. As well as objective distance, living in America meant that Panofsky was forced to master a language that was not his own. With its origins based in the German-speaking countries, the discipline of art history had created its own technical language, which even for those who spoke German, proved to be highly complex and difficult to understand. One term might have a great number of meanings resulting in rather abstract and vague terminology. Studying and writing art history in English turned out to be an unexpected advantage for Panofsky as the English art historical language was far more straight-forward, not least because American art historians were often obliged to write for, or lecture to, a nonprofessional audience. In his 1953 essay on being a European scholar in America, Panofsky explains how a less daunting vocabulary opened up opportunities for him and his peers to write books that dealt with entire periods of art history rather than merely specialized papers.

Finally, in 1935, a faculty for Humanistic Studies was opened at the Institute for Advanced Studies in Princeton where Panofsky became the first permanent professor. This opportunity to work and teach in a humanistic environment, which would not have been available to him had he stayed in Germany, meant that Panofsky was able to take his beliefs and ideas of how art history should be taught and studied in exactly the direction he wanted. According to his friend and colleague, William S. Heckscher, it was Panofsky's unconventional lectures and seminars, which might include French poetry and Ancient Greek history, for example, that made them truly exciting and revolutionary. From this liberating and auspicious place, Panofsky was to go on to make a marked influence on the direction that art history was to take.

3. A Science of Art

A year after writing his essay on perspective (see Chapter 2), Panofsky set about creating a method that was systematic in its approach. It was to be a sort of 'science of art'. Taking his criticisms of Wölfflin and Riegl as his point of departure, Panofsky turned to his ex-student, friend and colleague from Hamburg, Edgar Wind, for inspiration.

Edgar Wind

In 1925 Wind published his essay, 'Theory of Art vs. Aesthetics'. This essay was originally part of his doctoral thesis and had been written three years earlier under Panofsky's supervision. In this essay Wind presented a 'system' by which he believed it was possible to reveal how an artist made certain decisions in order to overcome artistic problems and, hence, produce the artwork in the way that he or she did.

Wind begins by examining the idea of an aesthetic object and its value, in other words, what is it and what is its significance? He concludes that an artwork is a self-sufficient, isolated object with no meaning other than its own, unless it is related to other things, at which point its meaning is changed. He uses the example of hanging a painting in a room. On its own the painting is one thing, but as soon as it is hung on the wall, it lends something to the room and the effect of what we see is something different. The painting and its surroundings become a new aesthetic phenomenon. Wind sees the value of an aesthetic object as being unique in the way it has an immediate quality that is not connected to anything else. There is nothing that gives the object value – it is part of the object's fundamental nature, something that is already there. This cannot be said for anything else in other fields, as usually one must have knowledge of an object before we can assess its value, or else the value is in the account itself that is given of the object. With an aesthetic object, however, we comprehend the value when we take in the object visually. The problem then, says Wind, is this: if the value of an aesthetic object is an isolated individual phenomenon, then how can its significance be proved?

Wind suggests that for an art historian who seeks the why and the how of the creation of an artwork, and for an art critic who seeks to judge a work's validity, the answer must be based on art theory. When looking at Wind's art theoretical method we can see how fundamentally important his concept was to Panofsky's own conceptual system for understanding the 'intrinsic value' of an artwork.

Wind's argument goes something like this: If we are to prove whether an aesthetic judgement is right or wrong, we must move from contemplation to analysis. Through analysis, the aesthetic object is, necessarily, dissected into parts so that

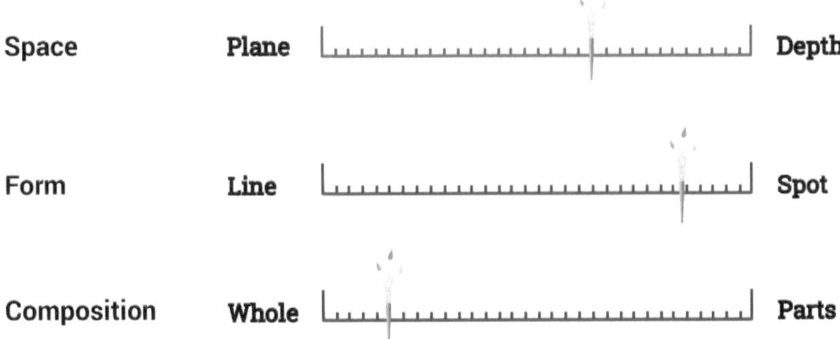

Fig. 8 Decisions on form automatically decide the outcome of space and composition.

what was initially a whole independent object now becomes an object made up of components (such as composition, space, and form). Since these components are common to other artworks, the object can now no longer be classed as isolated, and it is therefore possible to begin to establish connections.

In looking at a work of art, then, we move through several channels of thought. First, in contemplating an aesthetic object, we are prompted to make a statement about that object (which may be a simple statement about whether we like the painting or not). If the person contemplating the artwork is an art historian, a statement or query may arise about the artist's intention. This, in turn, may prompt an opposing statement, which precipitates a discussion. In this way, art contemplation becomes art criticism. And art criticism, says Wind, calls upon certain concepts that have their basis in art theory. By using art theory, an art historian can begin to clarify what artistic problems the artist came up against and how they made certain decisions in order to overcome them.

In the same way that a writer puts together words using grammar to make meaning, and adds concepts and logic to create understanding, the artist must put certain elements together in order to make a coherent artwork. The sorts of problems that an artist will have to solve are those concerning space, form and composition. Wind breaks these three elements down as follows: space: plane vs. depth; form: line vs. spot; and composition: the whole vs. parts (see Fig. 8).

Within his methodological system, Wind is not saying that an artist must deal with the different components in fixed ways, but that the artist's decision concerning one part of a problem will necessarily influence corresponding problems. For example, Impressionists of the 19th century favoured spot over line, which in turn meant that they had to go with depth in their work rather than plane. Looking at artworks in this way allows the art historian to analyse how and why the artist made the decisions they did.

Panofsky's Grundbegriffe (basic concepts)

The same year that Wind published 'Theory of Art vs. Aesthetics', Panofsky published his own ideas on a basic system of concepts for art history. His essay, 'On the Relationship of Art History and Art Theory: Towards the Possibility of a Fundamental System of Concepts for a Science of Art' (1925, translated in 2008), shows his determination to find his Archimedean viewpoint. It describes a method that begins with philosophical thought. Applied in a carefully structured way, this line of thought creates a framework for a more scientifically based art history relying upon fact. The basis is vastly indebted to Wind's study, whereby he takes the idea of the artistic object, with its own fundamental value, and looks at how it is subjected to a certain 'organizing' by the artist (of which certain artistic problems facing the artist must be solved). Although Panofsky was a contextualist, (see Chapter 2), at this point in the formulation of his theoretical method he was essentially focusing on form and style. It wasn't until his method developed to include iconography and iconology (which we will look at in detail in Chapter 4) that he put form and context together.

His essay is very much a follow-on from the one he wrote five years earlier in his critique of Riegl's kunstwollen (see Chapter 2). He sets out to determine the kunstwollen of an artistic object (remember that, for Panofsky, the kunstwollen meant the 'intrinsic value' of an object). In order to accomplish this, Panofsky came up with a set of criteria that combined art history (the more factual

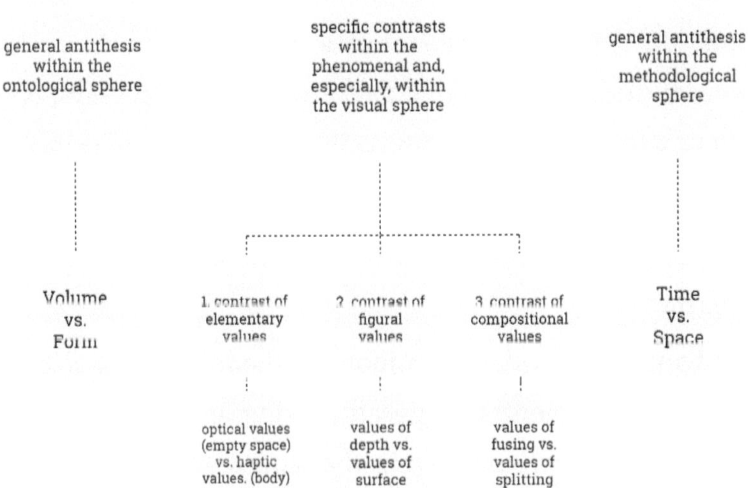

Fig. 9 Panofsky's schematic representation.

part concentrating on things that we can actually see in reality) with art theory (the theoretical part that includes concepts we arrive at through contemplating our observations).

Primary Concepts

Panofsky constructed a diagram (Fig. 9) in order to demonstrate the way he sees his theoretical concepts working. At first glance it is difficult to understand how it works, but Fig. 10 (see Secondary Concepts) should help clarify how all the values work together.

Panofsky looks at an artwork from two different angles – theoretical and scientific. Let's take a look at each in turn.

Theoretical

If looking at an artwork from a theoretical point of view, Panofsky explains, we could say that all artworks are fundamentally made up of a quantity of what he calls 'sensible perception'. What he means by this is an artist's artistic feeling, judgement or insight. He labels this *volume*. At the same time this 'volume of sensible perception' necessarily encounters a certain structuring, which Panofsky categorizes as *form*. Every work of art, he says, is the result of a happy balance between these two opposing principles. It is the structuring of that volume without destroying the feeling and perception.

Scientific

If studying an artwork from a more methodological or scientific angle, however, Panofsky suggests looking at the two opposing principles of *volume* and *form* in the same way we might regard *space* and *time*: space standing in for volume, and time standing in for form. He sees this comparison as being viable because the 'feeling' or 'perception' of an artwork (its volume) is something that is understood in its entirety, in the same way that we comprehend space. Whereas form relates to time in the way that it structures something abstract.

According to Panofsky, whichever way you look at an artwork – theoretically or scientifically – there is always the same fundamental contrasting concepts at the core of every piece of work: volume/space vs. form/time. Panofsky sees the theoretical concepts of volume and form as presenting the problem, in the manner of art theory, and the methodological, or scientific, take of space and time as proposing a solution, much in the way that art history and art criticism might. From these basic concepts, Panofsky came up with more specific contrasting pairs of concepts, which look a little closer at how the artwork comes into being.

Secondary Concepts

In between the theoretical concepts of volume and form, and the scientific concepts of space and time, Panofsky puts three more contrasting pairs. The first is optical vs. haptic, which basically represents 'empty space vs. substance'. He refers to this pair as the *elementary values* of an artwork, the balance of which creates an abstract pattern that we can't yet understand. Panofsky sees this as the visual representation of the volume vs. form antithesis. The second pair of concepts – depth vs. surface – refers to the *figural values* of an artwork and is when the abstract pattern starts to become something concrete that we can recognize. Panofsky

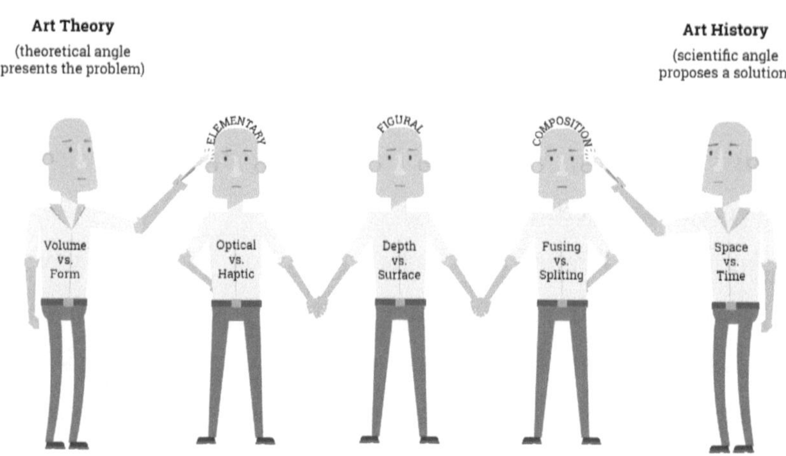

Fig. 10 The relationship between the primary and secondary concepts.

calls the third pair of concepts *compositional values*, which represent fusing vs. splitting. This is where the concrete forms are organized into some sort of composition. Panofsky sees the balance between fusing and splitting as the visual example of space vs. time (were it something tangible). He explains this by comparing time with forms fused together – neither of which can be split. He sees forms and time as both being something that come together in movement to form a whole. At the same time, he compares space with isolated forms, describing the way that neither have a sense of movement or of becoming a unity; both have only a sense of 'being' as an individual entity.

To help us understand better, let's look at this concept in context. We, as art historians, start with the so-called 'problem' – the 'why is it painted in that way?'. If we go back to the beginning, we must imagine the artist with a clean canvas and ideas in his or her head. By using artistic feeling, judgement and insight (volume), the artist must come up with a way of structuring (form) this inner creativity in order to create the first stage of the artwork (this is the point at which elementary values are implemented). To begin with, an abstract pattern begins to form as substance is added to the empty space (optical and haptic). As the artist continues, the second stage of the artwork begins to form (as figural values are implemented) while the artist contemplates the levels of depth and surface that are needed. The abstract forms are now becoming more concrete. As the artist moves towards the third stage (when compositional values are implemented), the artwork is completed and, from an art historian's point of view, the solution to the initial 'problem' comes to fruition. Having decided upon how much to bring forms together (fusing) and where they need to be placed separately (splitting), the artist has created a finished composition. The 'solution' is based upon the artist's decisions on balancing the pairs of values.

All three 'artistic problems' have to be solved at the same time – and are in fact one reliant upon the other. Whereas optical vs. haptic is the visual manifestation of volume vs. form, and fusing vs. splitting that of space vs. time, it is the middle figural value that plays the mediating role. For, in order for something concrete and recognizable to be created, the artist first needs to solve the problem between optical and haptic (empty space vs. body), which structures his or her feeling/intuition into an abstract pattern. Similarly, the figural value relies on the fusing vs. splitting concept in order for its concrete form to be organized into a composition (see Fig. 10).

Is This all Really Necessary?

Panofsky sets out to show that essentially the role of an art historian in terms of style (in a strict sense) is purely to collate and label what he calls the 'sensible qualities' of an artwork. What he means by this are those demonstrative or suggestive concepts that are the artist's resulting work, such as making colour solemn or cheerful, making cloth rustling or flowing etc. As it is essential that an art historian remain objective in the study of an artwork, the resulting classifications of the aspects of a work are usually expressed as 'the way the artist has depicted the hands' or 'the mode in which the folds of cloth have been composed'. What this means in terms of understanding an artwork, is that while the art historian can see that an artist has solved particular artistic problems and is able to describe the way in which the artist has gone about it based on the facts evident, it is the role of the art theorist to understand and suggest how. So, Panofsky argues, it makes complete sense for art history and art theory to work together, and using a fundamental system of concepts is the way it can be done.

Principles of Design & Stylistic Principles

The art historian is able to single out certain stylistic similarities or differences in works of art and can then classify them as belonging to a certain group. For example, in one painting the forms might be seen as pictorial (merging forms full of movement) as opposed to plastic (distinct lines creating a solid object). The art historian might then relate this painting to another using similar stylistic concepts. By doing so, the art historian is confirming that the artworks he groups together have similar principles of design, and therefore a corresponding underlying stylistic principle. But now he or she needs to get to the bottom of what those stylistic principles are and how the artist went about applying them.

When an artist sets out to paint a convincing 'rustling, velvety' robe, he or she must conform to certain rules in order to achieve this. The 'how to do this' is the initial artistic problem that the artist faces, and the stylistic criteria (such as deciding the extent of depth/surface or colour/polychrome etc.) is what the artist will engage with. These contrasting points of reference are what Panofsky describes as 'principles of design'. Each principle of design is in fact an individual stylistic principle that is the result of the artist deciding where on the scale between the two points he or she must stop. This resulting point is the unity of a pair of concepts and is the solution to the artistic problem.

So let's say that the art historian starts with the artistic problem: How did the artist create such a realistic looking velvety, rustling robe? He or she must then interpret the suggestive/demonstrative concepts (velvety, rustling) as these describe only the 'perceptible qualities' of an artwork. This he or she will do using the stylistic concepts commonly used in art history, such as 'this painting is pictorial with depth and movement in the folds of the cloth'. If the art historian were to incorporate art theory into his or her method, then he or she would go beyond simply interpreting what they see into a stylistic concept. They would look at this interpretation, Panofsky explains, as organizing each of these individual concepts into what he calls 'an internally connected complex'. In other words, each individual concept (which, as it is, describes the appearance of the artwork and is unconnected to anything but itself) is changed into something that is more like a system with a function (i.e. giving depth or adding movement).

The art historian would now start to look at these 'systems' as principles of design, which are not used randomly but are used together in order to create a particular style. Seen in this way, the art historian can work out that the artist created a pictorial work by veering closer to the optical values on the scale, which would cause the forms to merge and create a sense of movement. This merging of forms means that the artist has favoured the values of fusing over splitting when creating the composition of the work. From a more scientific view, the emphasis is with time rather than space, as there is a feeling of *becoming* rather than *being*, and again there is movement in this becoming and fusing. When we look at the second of the contrasting values in Panofsky's table – the mediating pair – we can see that it is necessary for the artist to give more value of depth in his or her work, as the opposing value of surface would have no shadow. In this way, it is necessary for all values to be decided upon at the same time in order for the artist to come up with his or her artistic solution.

Kunstwollen

So, where does the kunstwollen come into all of this? Well, for Panofsky, if an art historian wants to move beyond simply understanding the features that show the existence of something to understanding what causes those features to be as they are, one must seek out the kunstwollen of an artwork. The kunstwollen

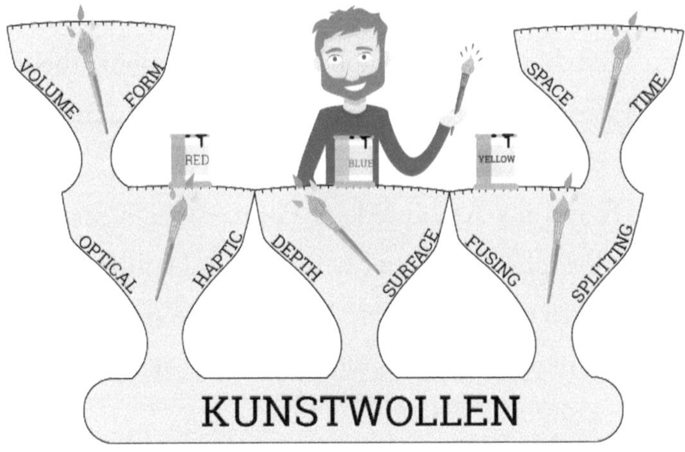

Fig. 11 The correct balance of contrasting concepts produces the 'kunstwollen'

– an artwork's 'internal sense', its very nature – is the resulting combination of all the artist's decisions regarding where to stop on the various scales for the contrasting concepts. It is a bit like making a potion: you start out with 'how do I do this?', then, after some experimentation and the harmonization of various components, the recipe is complete.

Art's Relationship with the Humanities

Panofsky was convinced that if it was possible to reveal the fundamental nature – the kunstwollen – of artistic phenomena, then it must also be possible for all other areas of the humanities. After all, philosophy, religion, linguistics, music, to name but a few, are all systems that have been created as solutions to problems. Individual cultures (be it determined by an era, a region or a people) tend to solve intellectual and artistic problems by way of the same ethos. Therefore, Panofsky proposes, it is entirely feasible that other areas of the humanities can be looked at as a 'science of things'. By making connections between first-hand observations and equivalent theoretical problems, a solution can be found that reveals the inner nature or sense of particular phenomena.

Having found his Archimedean Point – which provided the missing philosophical part to his formal and cultural method – Panofsky was to go on to create his tripartite system for which he was most renowned: that which combined both iconology and iconography.

4. Iconography and Iconology

Iconography entered the discipline of art history during the 19th century in the work of academics such as Anton Springer (1825–1891) and Émile Mâle (1862–1954). The focus during that time was on Christian religious art and the idea was to take the work of 16th- and 17th-century iconographers – which involved the classifying and organizing of subjects in the manner of an encyclopedia – and use it in a more scientific way in order to identify the motifs in works of art.

The term 'iconography' comes from the Greek word *eikonographia* – *eikon* meaning 'likeness', and *graphia* meaning 'describe by writing or drawing'. Art historians adopted this term to mean the visual description of symbols and the way they were thought to represent specific ideas, people or things. For example, in Western culture a cross is a symbol for Christianity and an obelisk represents dominance. The term 'iconology' has a slightly different meaning, in that its Greek derivation, *logos*, means 'word', 'thought' or 'reason'. In the 17th century, iconology was used to refer to a handbook that contained symbols for the use by artists who painted allegories. (An allegory is a story, poem or other work in which the characters and events represent certain religious, moral or political ideas.) In terms of iconology's use in the world of art history, it is about the historian going deeper than the face value of the symbol and studying it in its historical context. It is thought that the reason artists used symbols in their artwork (and continue to do so) is that it allows them to put a lot of information into each work without overwhelming the viewer.

Between 1932 and 1955, Panofsky had been defining his iconographical and iconological methods, the results of which were produced in his book *Studies in Iconology* and 'Iconography and iconology: an introduction to the study of Renaissance art' – an essay which he included in Meaning in the Visual Arts (1955). He was the first scholar to analyze the iconographical/ iconological methodology in such detail and his work was widely published and enthusiastically discussed. Panofsky redefined the way art historians used the term 'iconology'. It became the study that enables a historian to find the 'intrinsic meaning' or 'symbolic value' of an object – something that wasn't even necessarily intentionally created by the artist and therefore unknown to him or her. Panofsky believed that this intrinsic meaning had the potential to 'reveal the basic attitude of a nation, a period, a class, a religious or philosophical persuasion' (1955a). With his revision of iconology, he had moved the goalposts to include it into the branch of cultural history for the first time.

A Tripartite System

Let's start with a table that Panofsky constructed in order to summarize the different categories that he talks about (see Fig. 12). While the table refers to three different stages that the art

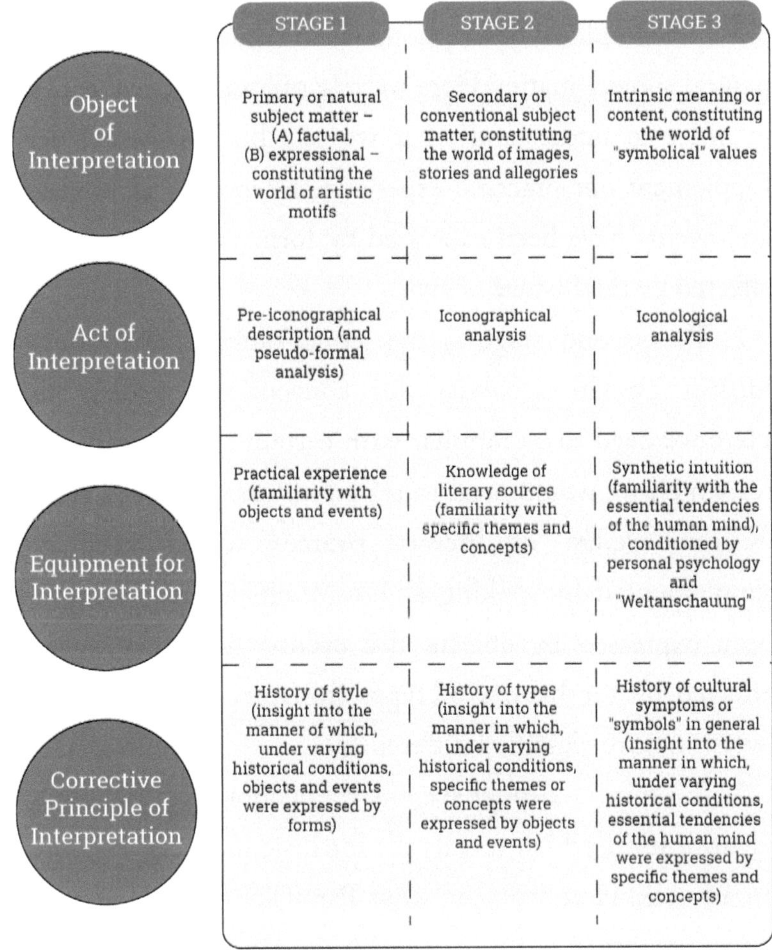

Fig. 12 Panofsky's synoptical table

historian would undergo through the course of his research, all refer to aspects of a work of art in its entirety. In other words, all parts merge to become one and the same methodological process.

Before explaining each section in detail, briefly we can see that Panofsky's method consists of three parts:

1. An art historian would begin his or her research with the pre-iconographical description, which focuses on the primary or natural subject matter. Here we rely on our practical experience in order to understand what we see. But we would need to supplement our practical experience by looking at how objects and events have been expressed by forms; how they have been affected by the history of style.

2. The second stage is the iconographical analysis, which focuses on the secondary or conventional subject matter. Here we need to be familiar with certain themes and concepts for which we would need to refer to literary sources. But again our knowledge of literary sources would need to be supplemented by looking at how themes and concepts have been expressed by objects and events; how they have been affected by the history of types (in other words, how things, over time, are classified differently).

3. The third and final stage is the iconological discovery and identification, which reveals the intrinsic meaning or content of an artwork. Here we need what Panofsky refers to as synthetic intuition, that is, a familiarity with the fundamental inclinations of the human mind. This can be verified by looking at the history of cultural symptoms or symbols. In other words, looking to see if the same tendencies are apparent in other areas of contemporary culture, such as politics, religion, philosophy etc.

Now let's go through the table in a bit more detail by putting the above in context. To explain the first two parts of each stage, Panofsky uses an everyday scene (albeit rather an old fashioned one now) of a man lifting his hat in greeting on the street. Panofsky's aim is to show the distinction between a formalistic reading of an artwork and one that concerns itself with the subject matter, which is where iconography comes in.

Initial Interpretation

Stage 1

From a purely formal point of view, if we imagine a man greeting us in the street we would see a grouping of details consisting of colour, lines and volumes. The movement (of the man lifting his hat) would constitute a slight change in the details. This is what we see formally.

As soon as we identify the grouping of details as an object (which is a man) and the change in those details as an event (the man is lifting his hat), then we have moved beyond simply looking at what is in front of us in a formal manner. We are now dealing with subject matter and meaning – a pre-iconographical description. Panofsky calls this initial, easily understandable meaning, the factual meaning. Basically, it is the way we identify forms with objects that are already known to us from our experience in life, and the way they change with particular events or actions.

The next part is what Panofsky calls the expressional meaning. This goes further than simply identifying forms and events – there is now the addition of empathy that relies on our sensitivity towards what we see based on our life-experience. What we see will naturally produce some sort of reaction within us: is the man's gesture friendly, aggressive, or indifferent?

Together, the factual meaning and the expressional meaning make up the first part of the content: the primary or natural subject matter.

Stage 2

Next Panofsky moves on to the second part of his tripartite method: the iconographical part which he labels the secondary or conventional subject matter. Here, to glean any further understanding from what we see in front of us, we must not only have knowledge of the objects and events around us, but also be familiar with the customs and cultural traditions that are specific to what we see. If you are from the Western world, you will know that a man lifting his hat is in fact a greeting and a gesture of politeness. (What you may or may not know is that this action is a leftover gesture from mediaeval times when armed men would take off their helmets as a signal of peace.) For those living in very different civilizations, it might not be apparent that a man lifting his hat is in fact a polite greeting. Therefore, there is an element of understanding needed for this part of the method.

Stage 3

The final part of the method requires us to look beyond the visible and intelligible actions of the man. To enact an iconological reading of the man lifting his hat, we must bring together various pieces of information that will help us to understand his very nature. Firstly, for example, all the things that have conditioned him, such as the age he is living in, the part of the world he comes from, his social and educational background, and details of his past life and present environment. And secondly, what we might call the man's 'philosophy' – his individual way of looking at things and his personal reaction to the world he lives in.

Separately each action that the man makes, or each individual observation that we make of him, only hints at who he is, and therefore it is not possible to formulate a comprehensive account of the man solely through his action of lifting his hat. However, if we were to interpret the hat-lifting action alongside a large number of other, comparable observations, and with reference to the man's class, nationality, intellectual and cultural traditions etc., then we can begin to create a complete picture of the man's character. It is only then, once we have the whole picture, that it becomes clear that the man's personality is subtly embedded into each individual action/observation.

Panofsky calls this third stage the intrinsic meaning or content and refers to it as 'essential', by which he means fundamental to human nature. The first two stages he describes as 'phenomenal', that is to say that it is perceptible through our senses or through direct experience. For Panofsky, the intrinsic meaning acts as a unifying principle – an 'all-encompassing truth', if you like. It determines the form (the man's personality affects his outward appearance) and it both causes and explains the event and its significance (the fundamentals of who he is causes his polite gesture and explains why he chooses this particular action).

The Right Equipment for the Job

In order to explain how we can take this process further, Panofsky uses an example of a 17th-century Venetian painting by an artist

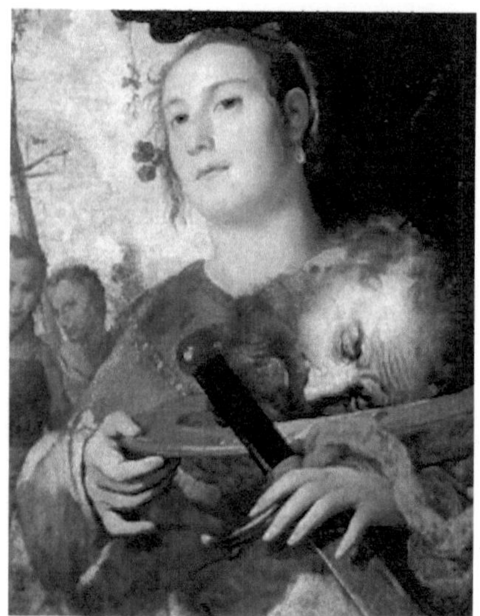

Fig. 13 *Judith* by Francesco Maffei, , c. 1650–60, Pinacoteca Comunale de Faenza, Faenza, Italy.

called Francesco Maffei (see Fig. 13). The painting portrays a young woman holding a large flat dish on which rests a dead man's head. In her left hand she holds a sword.

In the early 1900s, this particular painting was subject to some confusion as to the identity of the woman. As art historians, practical experience of religious paintings would indicate to us that the woman represents Salome, the daughter of Herod II and Herodias, who appears in the New Testament as demanding and receiving the head of St. John the Baptist on a dish (referred to back then as a 'charger'). But knowledge of literary sources, such as the Bible, would tell us that she did not decapitate St John the Baptist herself, and therefore the fact that she is holding a sword casts some doubt. The Book of Judith, included in the Old Testament, refers to another young woman, a Jewish widow called Judith. In the story, she goes to the enemy camp with her maid where she proceeds to ingratiate herself with the general, Holofernes. After winning his trust, she decapitates him and takes his head back to her fellow countrymen. The appearance of the man's head and the sword in the painting would appear to fit this theme. But in the reverse of the above, the charger does not.

So we have the head and charger, which fit the theme of Salome, and the head and sword, which fit the theme of Judith. But both are questionable.

However, this is where we would supplement our practical experience by looking at the history of style; how, across time, certain objects and events are expressed in different forms. So we would look back to other portrayals of Judith and Salome that were painted before Maffei's depiction. We would look for examples that are not in doubt, such as a painting where Salome is depicted with her parents or Judith is shown with her faithful maid. If we find accepted examples where Salome has a sword or Judith has a charger, it indicates which woman Maffei's depiction is most likely to be. Panofsky verifies that there is not a single work showing Salome with a sword, but there are several 16th-century examples in both Germany and Northern Italy that show Judith with a charger.

To further convince ourselves that Maffei's painting is of Judith, we could investigate the history of types in order to learn how certain themes and concepts use different objects and events depending on the historical time in which they are being depicted. Here we would hope to find out why the motif of a charger could be switched from the theme of Salome to that of Judith, but not the motif of the sword from Judith to the theme of Salome. Panofsky confirms that if we were to research how things come to be classified differently over time, we would learn that the motif of a sword is a recognized symbol for Judith, representing virtues such as Justice and Fortitude. Salome, on the other hand, is often depicted as representing a dangerous female seductress.

Therefore, a motif of virtues would be a wholly inappropriate and entirely unlikely representation for Salome. However, during the 14th and 15th centuries, the image of the head of St. John the Baptist on a charger had become a devotional symbol in itself, separate from any context, particularly in Northern Italy and Germany. Consequently, if an artist from that time were planning to paint a beheaded man, he would be familiar with the association of a charger with the image of a head. Hence, in a devotional painting, the sack that Judith used to carry the head back to her people could conceivably be substituted for a charger.

When it comes to the final iconological part of Panofsky's method, texts referring to the histories and depictions of Salome or Judith will not be able to provide us with the information we need in order to discover the intrinsic meaning of the artwork. What we are looking for is something that will reveal the basic principles that underlie the artist's choices and finished work. So far we have asked ourselves the following questions: Why did the artist choose those specific artistic motifs (forms)? Why did he or she present those motifs in such a way? How have those motifs been interpreted as images, stories and allegories? These questions deal with the work of art specifically. However, by looking at forms, motifs, images, stories and allegories as the basic attitude of an artist, a nation, a period etc. made visible, we are interpreting these manifestations of expression as symbolic forms in the same way that Cassirer did (see Chapter 2). In order to grasp the intrinsic meaning of the work, Panofsky tells us that we need to exercise what he calls 'synthetic intuition'. However, because anything relying on 'intuition' will be affected by our own psychology and by what Panofsky calls our *Weltanschauung* (which translates as our 'worldview'), a corrective principle is once again needed. In the same way that our practical experience needed to be supplemented with looking at the history of style, and our knowledge of literary sources supplemented with the history of types, our synthetic intuition must be expanded to include the history of cultural symptoms or symbols. That is to say, that we must look at, not only the fundamental way that a human mind expresses itself by means of themes and concepts, but how that can differ considerably at specific points in history. In other words, we must look at the history of tradition.

We can do this by checking what we consider to be the cultural features in an artwork alongside as many other historical documents as possible that originate from the same period of time. These could be any documentation that gives us some idea of how a civilization, a country, a specific person, or a particular period in time, worked in terms of its politics, its religion, its philosophical tendencies, its scientific leanings, and other art forms such as poetry and theatre. Here we can see Panofsky's humanistic discipline in practice.

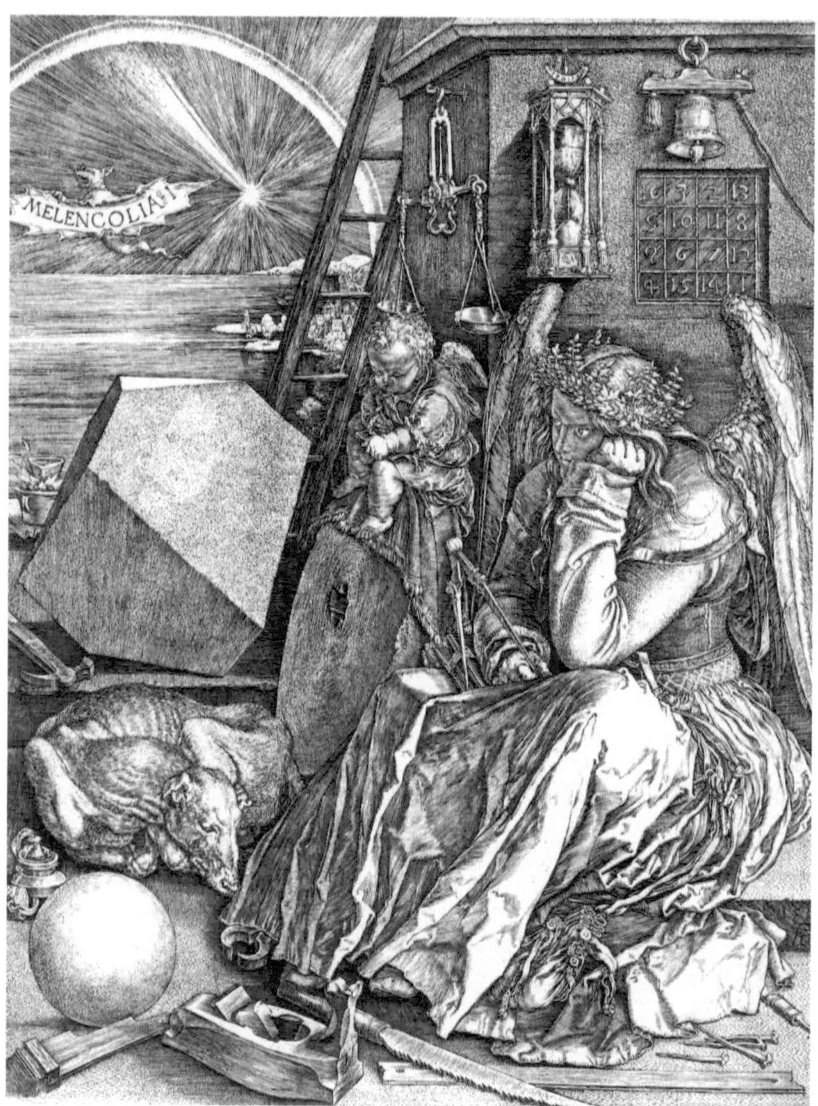

Fig. 14 *Melencolia I* by Albrecht Dürer (1514)

5. Method in Action

The engraving opposite is that which Panofsky studied alongside Fritz Saxl when they took over the project from Aby Warburg in 1923 (see Chapter 2). Later on Panofsky included their results in *The Life and Art of Albrecht Dürer* (1943) where we can see the application of his tripartite method used on *Melencolia I*. If we break Panofsky's study down into the three different stages – pre-iconographical, iconographical and iconological – we can see how Panofsky's method uncovers the more hidden cultural traditions present at the time the painter made the work.

Stage 1: Pre-iconographical

Beginning with the pre-iconographical stage, let us look at Dürer's engraving in the manner that Panofsky's method would demand. What we see are two winged figures; a woman and a child, with an emaciated dog, sitting next to a building by the sea, surrounded by various objects – some recognizable to us and others not. In order to take this description further, we must use our practical experience of the world to establish certain facts. For example, Christmas or religious traditions would lead us to believe that the woman is an angel and the child a cherub or cupid (if we were knowledgeable about Renaissance art, we would know that this infant is in fact called a putto). We would assume that the time of day is night as the sky is dark and there is what must be a comet clearly visible in the sky. We can assume that this is a comet and not a star by the tail streaming upwards away from where the sun has set. We might spot that the moon is likely to be bright from the shadow cast by the hourglass on the wall. Our knowledge of human emotions would indicate to us that neither figure looks particularly happy, in fact the woman looks miserable, with her head on her hand in what we recognize as an expression of feeling despondent. Further evidence of this is the word 'melencolia' (an ancient spelling) written across a flying bat's wings, leading us to believe that the engraving is illustrating the theme of melancholy.

But what of the objects scattered around the figures – what have they to do with melancholy? Looking closely they appear to be tools that a carpenter or builder might use – a plane, a hammer, a saw, a ruler, some nails etc. The other objects – the sphere and the large multi-faceted block resting next to the ladder, the compass in the woman's hand and the numbered square above her head – all suggest something more mathematical. Here we find ourselves applying Panofsky's corrective principle – the history of styles, which allows us to understand how objects are expressed by forms – in order to interpret what we see. But from here we must move on to the next stage and subject the engraving to an iconographical analysis.

Stage 2: Iconographical

Whereas in the first stage we identified the artistic motifs, for the second stage we must refer to literary sources in order to interpret what part those motifs play in the bigger picture. In other words, in the world of images, stories and allegories, do these motifs form part of a specific theme or concept?

The Four Humours

According to Panofsky, at the time that Dürer produced his engraving, the word 'melancholy' wasn't yet used as an expression for 'feeling gloomy'. The clue to what it did mean back in the 15th century is in the word itself, deriving via late Latin from the

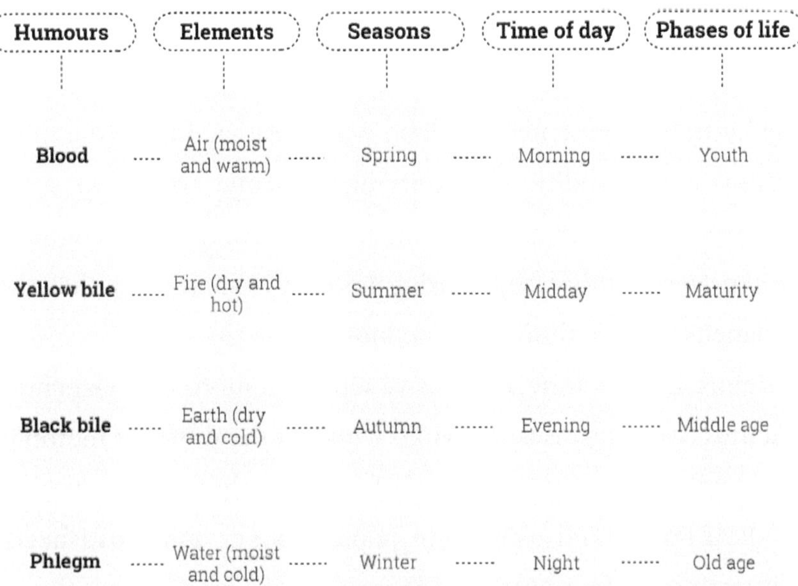

Fig. 15 The Four Humours

Greek *melankholia*: '*melan*' meaning 'black' and '*kholē*' meaning 'bile'. Black bile points to the Ancient Greek system of medicine, known as the 'four humours' which represent the four bodily fluids in a person, an excess or deficiency of which was thought to directly affect a person's temperament and health. An excess of black bile was believed to cause depression, hence how the word melancholy was to become an expression for sadness or depression in more modern-day English.

Panofsky's study of the four humours reveals that they were thought to work in harmony alongside the four elements, the four seasons, the four times of day and the four phases of life. By the end of classical Antiquity and into the Middle Ages, it was thought that one of the humours shown in the table (see Fig. 15) was prominent in each person, determining everything about that person, from their appearance to their personality. While the humour represented by blood was considered to be the most fortunate of conditions, signifying someone with a positive temperament, black bile was the most feared. It was thought to be the worst of diseases, causing insanity – something that the melancholic were thought to be most prone to.

Before Dürer's time, illustrative representations of melancholy fell into two categories: drawings showing the different methods of treatment for the 'condition' of melancholy that appeared in medical books; and pictures in popular books and broadsheets, illustrating the four humours. These were of a more descriptive or dramatic nature and appeared in two different styles. One style showed figures differing by age, social status and profession, and might, for example, show the positive temperament as a young, well-dressed falconer standing on a cloud (to indicate the element of air). Whereas the melancholic was usually shown as an older, miserable miser standing on solid ground (to indicate the element of earth), clutching a purse and standing next to a desk covered in coins. The second style depicted figures in pairs, showing their temperament by their behaviour. Panofsky describes the most popular portrayal of the melancholic in medieval writing as being miserable and lethargic, which was based on the idea of sinful sleep – sloth or 'Acedia' being one of the seven deadly sins. So for example, the illustrations might show a woman asleep by her spindle and a man having dozed off at his desk.

Geometry

After identifying the theme of the four humours, Panofsky went on to look at the objects scattered around the figure, in order to shed light on the theme of geometry that clearly played a part in Dürer's engraving.

Before we look at Panofsky's observations, however, it is helpful to do a little research ourselves in order to understand the background to his thinking. From the time of classical antiquity through to about 1600, the 'arts' (as defined by Aristotle to include 'every productive effort based on a rational principle') were separated into two groups. There were the seven liberal arts – grammar, logic, rhetoric, arithmetic, geometry, theory of music and astronomy – which were skills considered essential for the 'learned' man, and practised by university scholars and humanist intellectuals. Then there were the mechanical arts, which represented tradesmen, which in those days included painters, sculptors and architects, as well as tailors, weavers, agriculturalists, masons, blacksmiths etc. In short, anyone who worked with their hands was included in this category, and was considered by intellectuals to be an uneducated plebeian artisan. This social division was still very much in place during Dürer's time and, as is evident from the writings of contemporary artists, was a point of contention amongst painters and sculptors. They argued that alongside painting and sculpting, there is a requirement for learning perspective and geometry and therefore their profession should be included in the liberal arts.

Panofsky's research into the theme of geometry reveals that, beginning in the middle of the 12th century, the 'arts' (as described above) became a popular subject for artists, sculptors and craftsmen alike. First the seven liberal arts took precedent, then the mechanical arts followed suit. Panofsky notes that, in all subjects, images followed the same composition. Whether individually or collectively, the arts were represented by a central female figure, sometimes alongside a secondary figure. Surrounding these characters would have been objects that symbolized the activity

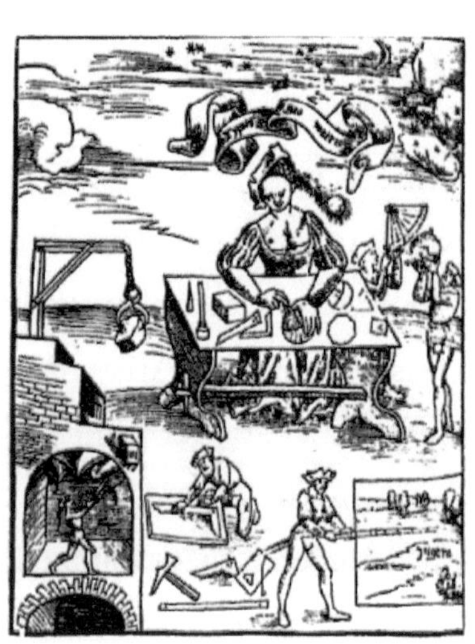

Fig. 16 *Typus Geometriae, Margarita Philosophica* (1504 and 1508), Gregor Reisch

being represented, with the most typical being held by the figure herself. So it would seem that, in *Melencolia I*, Dürer is following a well-known composition. Panofsky unearths an example of one such illustration in one of the most popular encyclopedias of Dürer's time – the *Margarita philosophica* by Gregor Reisch. The illustration in question is a woodcut entitled *Typus Geometriae* and includes many objects that also appear in Dürer's *Melencolia I*.

From the illustration (Fig. 16), we can see that *Typus Geometriae* shows a woman as the central figure, measuring a sphere with a compass. There are various instruments used by draftsmen scattered around on the table and on the floor, including an inkpot, a hammer and a ruler. The theme of astronomy also appears in the woodcut, symbolized by the two men to the right of the female figure, making astronomical measurements using a quadrant and an astrolabe (instruments commonly used in the 15th century). The peacock's feather in the woman's hat is an ancient symbol for a starry sky, as can be seen above her head.

In *Melencolia I*, the female central figure holds a compass with a sphere at her feet, while other objects of a similar nature to those in *Typus Geometriae* lie round about. According to Panofsky, the book, the inkpot and the compass represent pure geometry; the hourglass, scales, magic square and bell represent measurement in space and time; the technical instruments at Melencolia's feet represent applied geometry; and finally the large many-sided block next to the ladder represents descriptive geometry, that is to say, perspective and stereography (the representation of something that is 3D onto a 2D surface). From the iconographical identification of these geometrical objects, it is clear that Dürer set out to, not only illustrate one of the four humours, but to illustrate the liberal art of geometry in the manner that was typical in his day.

Astronomy and Astrology

The lunar rainbow encircling the comet in Dürer's engraving refers to the art of astronomy and adds credence to the idea that Dürer is including the theme of the liberal arts in his work. In Fig. 17, we can see how the comet itself appears to play the role of the vanishing point used in the mathematical art of linear perspective. The viewer's eye is drawn along several lines: from the compass in the woman's hand; the left-edge of the multi-faceted block; and the overhang of the building. All give a geometrical feel to the composition.

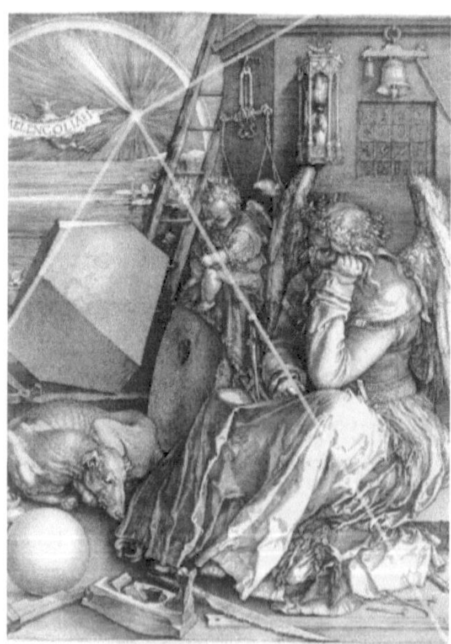

Fig. 17 Using mathematics in art.

Before the 17th century, astronomy and astrology were considered together, so it doesn't appear unconnected when, in Panofsky's identification of the various objects lying about in *Melencolia I*, we learn that the magic square inset into the wall above the woman's head isn't a mathematical magic square at all. It is infact a mensula Jovis – an astrological talisman. In

Dürer's time, the seven planets were thought to be connected to the four temperaments. Jovis refers to the planet Jupiter, which was associated with the favoured humour represented by blood, spring and youth. The melancholy humour was associated with the planet Saturn, hence the meaning of the word 'saturnine' (gloomy). Dürer's inclusion of the mensula Jovis therefore could be meant to ward off worries, fear and misery.

Theory and Practice

Panofsky looks a little closer at the motifs of the keys and purse that hang from Melencolia's belt. According to Panofsky the purse is the symbol of a miser, which is one of the characteristics of melancholy and the keys, too, can be connected to this theme. One of the sketches that Dürer made for his engraving included the words 'Key denotes power, purse denotes wealth'. From the shabby way that these objects hang from Melencolia's belt, Panofsky concludes that her power and wealth have been reduced in some capacity and wonders what meaning could be behind this. In Dürer's theoretical writings, Panofsky finds references to Dürer's belief that wealth is the rightfully earned reward for an artist and that power (by which is meant 'complete mastery') is the ultimate goal for an artist to reach in his work. Dürer sees these two attributes as being possible only through the mastering of two things: theoretical insight (for example, knowledge of geometry and perspective); and practical skill. If an artist possesses both these abilities, then they become 'ingenious'.

We are beginning to gain insight into the world of images and allegories that Dürer would have been privy to. The figure of the woman in Dürer's engraving, looking miserable with her head propped against her hand and her purse and keys hanging from her belt in a rather neglected fashion, begins to make sense now that we are acquainted with the themes described above. The emaciated dog and the bat are further evidence of melancholia as they are both traditionally associated with this theme, as is the astrological talisman warding off dark humour. Panofsky sees the inclusion of the scribbling putto as a device to emphasize the inaction of the woman, symbolizing the failed union of theory and practice. Melencolia thinks but is unable to act, and the putto, by scribbling away on his slate, represents practical skill that acts but does not think. This lack of harmony creates misery for Melencolia.

Melancholia Redefined

However, unusually for that time, Dürer has depicted his Melencolia as one who is not lazy, but has become immobilized by the futility of life. In his revision of the theme of melancholy, he has changed the negative characteristics associated with the melancholic, such as laziness, spite, greed and disrespect, and introduced a concept more closely linked with creative genius. The surroundings of his Melencolia imply that she has the intelligence and creativity to think, invent and build, with the tools of geometry and carpentry scattered around her and the book and compass in her lap. But she has come to a standstill having been driven to despair and inaction by some insurmountable obstacle. As well as presenting melancholy in a different way, Dürer has also introduced the theme of geometry.

By synthesizing these two iconographical themes and revising the way each is usually represented, Dürer has created a new iconographical theme. Panofsky describes it as an 'Artist's Melancholy': by intellectualizing melancholy and at the same time humanizing geometry, which had previously only been represented in treatises and encyclopedias, Dürer has given both themes psychological meaning. But what prompted him in this innovative merging of themes, and what does it mean? In order to understand Dürer's choices, we must move on to the third stage of Panofsky's tripartite method.

Stage 3: Iconological

In the third stage of his analysis, Panofsky is seeking the intrinsic meaning of *Melencolia I*. What he must use for this (see Panofsky's synoptical table in Chapter 4) – is 'synthetic intuition' (familiarity with the essential tendencies of the human mind). In other words, he needs to look for evidence of Dürer's contemporaries expressing themselves in a similar way in what could be seen as cultural symptoms of 15th-century Germany. He does this by looking at other social and intellectual activities in the Middle Ages with a view to finding what he calls a 'thread of tradition which went into the fabric of Dürer's composition' (1955b).

The Influence of the Planets

Beginning with Dürer's revision of the theme of melancholy, Panofsky sets out to find evidence of a similar train of thought amongst Dürer's contemporaries. He comes across Marsilio Ficino (1433–1499), one of the most influential humanist philosophers of the Italian Renaissance. Ficino was the leader of the Neo-Platonic Florentine Academy, which set out to reintroduce Plato's ideas to Western Europe. In his treatises he reversed the whole concept of melancholy. Dürer was certainly aware of his work as he quotes Ficino in his own writings in 1512.

Ficino was himself a melancholic, which is probably why he sought to put a positive slant on this most feared of conditions. In his books on medicine and astrology, he takes up the ideas of Aristotle who described melancholics as walking on a knife-edge facing either over-stimulation or paralysis of thought. If they managed equilibrium between these two conditions, then the result of their achievements would be far superior to those of ordinary humans. The Florentine Neo-Platonists took this idea further by linking Aristotle's theory to that of Plato's 'divine frenzy', whereby a poet or artist would go into a higher state, embodying thoughts of the gods. Before long, the melancholic disposition took on an almost divine status and melancholy was thought to signify genius.

Dürer's inclusion of astrological and astronomical symbolism in *Melencolia I* was certainly a cultural symptom of the 15th century. The seven planets were thought to correspond to the four humours, as we touched upon in the Iconographical section, and it was Saturn that was associated with the melancholic temperament. The Florentine Neo-Platonists, taking their lead from the Ancient Greek philosopher Plotinus, regarded Saturn as one of the superior planets, believing it to symbolize intellect as opposed to practicality. Despite the continued belief in

Saturn's malignant nature, Ficino counselled that if one could focus on the divine contemplation that Saturn symbolized, then it was possible to escape the negative aspects of its influence and benefit from its divine power.

Panofsky also found a link between Saturn and geometry in several 15th-century manuscripts on astrology, whereby it was believed that the planet Saturn sent spirits to teach geometry. This concept was illustrated by Jacob de Gheyn's print *The Melancholic Temperament* (1596–97) which shows Saturn in human form clutching a compass and sphere, with his head in his hand in the exact manner of Dürer's Melencolia.

Melancholy and Geometry

Next Panofsky set out to find a link between melancholy and geometry, looking for evidence of other occurrences of the pairing of these two themes during the 15th century. Turning to another Italian philosopher in Dürer's time, Panofsky comes across the work of Pico della Mirandola (1463–1494). In his writings, Mirandola extensively discusses the ideas of the 13th-century scholastic philosopher Henry of Ghent (1217–1293), who had made a psychological connection between melancholy and geometry. Mirandola enthusiastically advocates Ghent's belief that there are two kinds of thinkers: those that do so in terms of solid mental images (what we might think of as vertical thinking) and those that are open to more abstract ideas (what we call lateral thinking). Ghent describes those that think in a more vertical manner as being melancholics. He believed that this characteristic gave them an aptitude to be the best mathematicians because they think in a very systematic and methodical way that follows one isolated point to its conclusion. On the other hand, he sees them as being very bad 'metaphysicians', as they are unable to think in a more open and creative manner.

If we look at it the other way round, Panofsky suggests, then does it not follow that gifted geometricians are likely to be melancholics due to their never being able to move beyond that strict linear way of thinking? If we are to apply this character type to Dürer's Melencolia, then we have one who can invent, build and think, but who is unable to go beyond that which belongs in the world of physical phenomena. She cannot understand abstract ideas and this inability has rendered her inactive, giving up even that which she is good at.

From here Panofsky moves on to a different literary source – that of Cornelius Agrippa of Nettesheim (1486–1535) who was also active in the same years as Dürer. Agrippa was a writer, theologian and physician and was famous for his book *De Occulta Philosophia* (The Hidden Philosophy, 1531). The original manuscript was known to have been circulated amongst German humanists in around 1510. It included subjects such as astrology and geomancy (the art of placing buildings auspiciously) and followed Marsilio Ficino's Neo-Platonic beliefs of the effects that cosmic forces can have on man. Agrippa believed that the universe gave man 'inspiration' either in the form of prophetic dreams, through deep reflective thought, or through melancholy, brought about through the influence of Saturn (see The Four Humours). He advocated that the three faculties of 'imagination', 'reason' and 'mind' could become exceptional under Saturn's influence, rendering the person a genius.

Whereas Neo-Platonic teachings had previously designated the dual role of melancholy and genius to theologians, poets and philosophers (all belonging to the liberal arts), Agrippa had revised this theory to include artists. He split the three faculties into three different levels, the first classifying those melancholics with the power of imagination to be artists and craftsmen. The second level declares those who are melancholic and possess the gift of reason to be scientists, physicians and statesmen. The third, and most revered, belonged to theologians. With a melancholic yet intuitive mind they were thought to be superior to the other faculties. Panofsky suggests that the 'I' in the title for Dürer's engraving – *Melencolia I* – follows Agrippa's classification system, representing the first, and least prestigious of geniuses.

Intrinsic Meaning

So what does this all mean? Well, according to Panofsky, *Melencolia I* was the first representation of the concept of melancholy to be changed from a scientific theme (the four humours) to an illustration of the 'arts'. If we look at Panofsky's research as a whole, it tells us that the 15th century experienced a form of evolution in terms of philosophical thought: Ficino and his Neo-Platonists turned the concept of melancholy on its head; Agrippa revised the theory of the dual role of melancholy and genius by including artists (who had previously been denied a place amongst the liberal artists); and Mirandola, via the teachings of Ghent, sought to connect the idea of genius to the otherwise negative state of melancholy.

Dürer, by creating a new iconographical theme himself, would appear to be following a general 15th-century philosophy. By combining melancholy and geometry, Dürer found a way of representing the frustrations of artists, who strive to achieve mastery in their work by attempting to strike a balance between intellect, imagination and skill. And if they fail, they fall victim to melancholia.

But Panofsky also saw Dürer's engraving as 'the subjective confession of an individual man' (1955b). According to Dürer's writings, he too was a melancholic, striving to find perfection in his work, but often becoming subject to 'darkness' and failure. He was also an artist-geometrician, representing a typical 15th-century artist who engages with both practical skill and mathematical theory, is inspired by the influence of the planets but struggles with 'human frailty and intellectual finiteness'. So not only does *Melencolia I* act as a voice for 15th-century Renaissance man, but it is Dürer's own voice telling us about himself.

Conclusion: Where to Now?

Panofsky's method requires extensive research into all areas of life in order to adequately prove that an artwork is the result of its zeitgeist. It is a brilliant method, but if any criticism can be levelled at Panofsky here, it is that he doesn't quite fulfill this requirement, as his research doesn't go further than looking at the writings of philosophers and 15th-century writers. However, as Michael Ann Holly suggests in her study of Panofsky (1984), his iconological stage should not necessarily be thought of as a final stage, but instead as a beginning. Panofsky's study of *Melencolia I* is open to endless research that could go in every direction, in much the way of Aby Warburg and his research group. To give you an idea of how to go about taking Panofsky's method further, let's take a brief look at other areas of activity during the late Middle Ages and early Renaissance and see if Dürer's engraving shows other cultural symptoms of the 15th century.

Time for a Change

Regarding this period of time as a whole, we know that the Renaissance saw some important changes during the span of its history. The Middle Ages is distinguishable by its feudal society, which was ruled by custom and tradition and relied upon collective-mindedness. However, all that changed with the advent of early capitalism in around 1500. Technology progressed rapidly and science was born and, in particular, mathematics. With the new demand for measurement and calculation, treatises on geometry and arithmetic were produced; Dürer's being one such example. So straightaway we can see that Dürer's engraving not only illustrates this cultural change in its inclusion of the theme of geometry – a subject that wasn't relevant in a feudal society – but also in the veering away from a culture of collective-mindedness to embrace the individualism of a new society.

This individualism and inventing of new patterns can be found in other areas of early capitalist culture across Germany, notably in art historian Michael Baxandall's study of limewood sculptors and the 'meistersingers' of Renaissance Germany. Baxandall looks at how these arts reflect contemporary cultural history, whereby craftsmen suddenly seemed to feel that it was insufficient to simply copy the way in which the old masters worked, and instead, in order to become a true master, decided that they must create their own new patterns of work. We learn that at the same time that Dürer was creating his own iconographical theme by synthesizing the themes of geometry and melancholy, the meistersingers were beginning to buck against the extremely conservative traditions of writing words to a time-honoured tune. From the 1480s onwards it became more and more common for meistersingers to create a new 'pattern' by writing an entirely original song, tune and verse-form of their own. Similarly, German poets were also transforming theory and practice, creating their own revolution with new patterns of rhythm and sound. Sculpture, too, was taking a new turn: sculptors were creating their own personal patterns as well as including elements of the classical past. It was thought that in order to be seen as an exceptional individual – a 'master' – one must be an inventor and create a new individual style, much in the way that Cornelius Agrippa of Nettesheim advocated that those artists and craftsmen possessing the faculty of imagination could become exceptional, making them a genius.

A Mathematical Culture

In this period of change and invention, the introduction of calculating with numerals rather than using an abacus with counters was to play a big part in contemporary culture. Beginning in Italy, and later spreading further afield, geometry, arithmetic and proportion were used on a daily basis in commerce, in particular the Rule of Three – an arithmetical tool used to calculate geometric proportion. Naturally, artists and craftsmen also used this formula when dealing with proportion in the making and seeing of pictures. The Rule of Three was also used in musical and architectural theory, taking the form of the Pythagorean harmonic scale. Painters often left traces of geometry in their work by way of three-dimensional or geometrical forms as a device to capture the interest of an audience well equipped to detect them. In poetry, poets would create a framework for their composition by using arithmetically symmetrical plans. These examples show just how much a part of the culture mathematics became during the Renaissance period.

Just the Beginning

Finding continuity across 15th-century culture as evidence of a zeitgeist is a never-ending task and we have only just begun to touch upon it here. But with extensive research into other areas of life, such as politics, science and religion, for example, it isn't hard to imagine that Panofsky's method could reveal further proof of an artwork, such as Dürer's *Melencolia I*, being embedded with intrinsic meaning that can tell us much about the work, the artist and the era in which it was created.

While the discipline of art history has moved on considerably since Panofsky's time, his scholarship is still considered to be of great importance and continues to act as a reliable point of reference for students studying art history today. While Panofsky himself was always rather self-effacing about his role as a pioneer in the methodology of art history, his influence, reputation and considerable publications speak otherwise. Though he described himself as an 'eclectic' rather than an 'innovator', he has unarguably safeguarded and developed those invaluable traditions of art historical scholarship, bringing them from their origins of German-speaking Europe to the rest of the world. He has taken what was an exclusive discipline and cultivated and communicated it to a much wider audience.

By developing his humanistic methodology, Panofsky sought to 'humanize' the practice of art history, over-riding abstract theory and offering instead a more practical form of art scholarship. In turn, what this offers aspiring art historians today is an opportunity to take Panofsky's humanistic discipline and continue to develop it to see just how far such an all-embracing practice can take us.

Bibliography

Works by Panofsky

Panofsky, Erwin (1955) *Meaning in the Visual Arts*, The University of Chicago Press.

Panofsky, Erwin (1925) Trs. by Jas Elsner and Katharina Lorenz 'On the Relationship of Art History and Art Theory: Towards the Possibility of a Fundamental System of Concepts for a Science of Art', *Critical Inquiry*, Vol. 35, No. 1 (Autumn 2008), pp. 43–71.

Panofsky, Erwin (1934) 'Jan van Eyck's Arnolfini Portrait', *The Burlington Magazine for Connoisseurs*, Vol. 64, No. 372 (Mar 1934), pp. 117–119, 122–127.

Panofsky, Erwin (1932) Trs. by Jas Elsner and Katharina Lorenz 'On the Problem of Describing and Interpreting Works of the Visual Arts', *Critical Inquiry*, Vol. 38, No. 3 (Spring 2012), pp. 467–482.

Panofsky, Erwin (1955) *The Life and Art of Albrecht Dürer*, Princeton University Press.

Panofsky, Erwin (1927) Trs. by Christopher S. Wood (1991), *Perspective as Symbolic Form*, New York: Zone Books.

Panofsky, Erwin (1927) Trs. by Johanna Bauman, 'Reflections on Historical Time', *Critical Inquiry*, Vol. 30, No. 4 (Summer 2004), pp. 691–701.

Panofsky, Erwin, (1939) *Studies in Iconology: Humanistic Themes in the Art of the Renaissance*, Icon Editions, (this edition, 1972)Panofsky, Erwin, (1920) Trs. by Kenneth J. Northcott and Joel Snyder, 'The Concept of Artistic Volition', *Critical Inquiry* (Autumn 1981), pp. 17 33.

Panofsky, Erwin (1958) Trs. by Ernest C. Hassold, 'Wilhelm Vöge: A Biographical Memoir', *Art Journal*, Vol. 28, No. 1 (Autumn 1968), pp. 27–37.

Other works cited

Argan, Guilio Carlo and Rebecca West (1975), 'Ideology and Iconology', *Critical Inquiry*, Vol. 2, No. 2 (Winter 1975), pp. 297–305

Bakos, Jan, (2014) 'Otto Pächt and Albert Kutal: Methodological Parallels', *Umeni Art*, No. 5, LXII, pp. 406–423.

Baxandall, Michael (1980) *The Limewood Sculptors of Renaissance Germany*, Yale University Press.

Baxandall, Michael (1988) *Painting and Experience in Fifteenth-century Italy*, Oxford University Press 2nd edn.

Berghahn, V. R. (1994) *Imperial Germany, 1871–1914: Economy, Society, Culture, and Politic*, Berghahn Books.

Bialostocki, Jan (1970) 'Erwin Panofsky (1892–1968): Thinker, Historian, Human Being', *Simiolus: Netherlands Quarterly for the History of Art*, Vol. 4, No. 2, pp. 68–89.

Boyer, Carl B., (1958) 'The Theory of the Rainbow: Medieval Triumph and Failure', *Isis*, Vol. 49, No. 4 (Dec 1958), pp. 378–390.

Brann, Noel L. (2002) *The Debate Over the Origin of Genius During the Italian Renaissance: The Theories of Supernatural Frenzy and Natural Melancholy in Accord and in Conflict on the Threshold of the Scientific Revolution*, The Netherlands: Brill.

Burckhardt, Jacob, (1860) *The Civilization of the Renaissance in Italy (1860).* 2 Vols. Ed. Benjamin Nelson and Charles Trinkaus. 1929. Reprint. New York, 1958.

Carrier, David (1989) 'Erwin Panofsky, Leo Steinberg, David Carrier: The Problem of Objectivity in Art Historical Interpretation', *The Journal of Aesthetics and Art Criticism*, Vol. 47, No. 4, pp. 333–347.

Carty, Carolyn M. (1985) 'Albrecht Dürer's Adoration of the Trinity: A Reinterpretation', *The Art Bulletin*, Vol. LXVII, No. 1 (Mar 1985), pp. 146–153.

Chanda, Jacqueline (1998) 'Art History Inquiry Methods: Three Options for Art Education Practice', *Art Education*, Vol. 51, No. 5, Critical Lenses (Sept 1998), pp. 17–24.

Doorly, Patrick (2004) '"Melencolia I": Plato's Abandoned Search for the Beautiful', *The Art Bulletin*, Vol. 86, No. 2 (June 2004), pp. 255–276.

Eckart, Goebel, Jerome Bolton and Sigrid Weigel (editors) (2013) *"Escape to Life": German Intellectuals in New York: A Compendium on Exile after 1933*, Berlin Boston: Walter de Gruyter GmbH & Co.

Elsner, Jas and Katharina Lorenz, (2012) 'The Genesis of Iconology', *Critical Inquiry*, Vol. 38, No. 3 (Spring 2012), pp. 483–512.

Gombrich, E. H. & Fritz Saxl (1970) *Aby Warburg: An Intellectual Biography*, London: Warburg Institute.

Gopnik, Adam (2015) 'In the Memory Ward', *The New Yorker*, 16 March issue.

Haag, Michael (2009) *The Rough Guide to The Lost Symbol*, Rough Guides Ltd.

Hart, Joan (1993) 'Erwin Panofsky and Karl Mannheim: A Dialogue on Interpretation', *Critical Inquiry*, Vol. 19, No. 3 (Spring 1993), pp. 534–566.

Hasenmueller, Christine (1978) 'Panofsky, Iconography, and Semiotics', *The Journal of Aesthetics and Art Criticism*, Vol. 36, No. 3, Critical Interpretation (Spring 1978), pp. 289–301.

Heckscher, William S. (1969) 'Erwin Panofsky: A Curriculum Vitae', *Record of the Art Museum, Princeton University*, Vol. 28, No. 1, Erwin Panofsky: In Memoriam, pp. 4–21.

Hegel, G. W. F. (1975) Trs. by T. M. Knox, *Aesthetics: Lectures on Fine Art Vol. 1*, Oxford University Press.Holly, Michael Ann (1984) *Panofsky and the Foundations of Art History*, Cornell University Press.

Institute for Advanced Study. Available at: www.ias.edu. [Accessed 12 Nov, 2018].

Keenan, Daniel (2014) 'Kultur and acculturation: Erwin Panofsky in the United States of America', PhD thesis, University of Glasgow.

Killy, Walther and Rudolf Vierhaus (editors) (2006) *Dictionary of German Biography (DGB): Thibaut-Zycha*, Vol. 10, München: K. G. Saur Verlag GmbH.

Levi, Albert William (1986) 'Kunstgeschichte als Geistesgeschichte: The Lesson of Panofsky', *Journal of Aesthetic Education*, Vol. 20, No. 4, (Winter 1986).

Levine, Emily J. (2013) *Dreamland of Humanists: Warburg, Cassirer, Panofsky, and the Hamburg School*, University of Chicago Press.

Levine, Emily J. (2011) 'PanDora, or Erwin and Dora Panofsky and the Private History of Ideas', *The Journal of Modern History*, Vol. 83, No. 4 (Dec 2011), pp. 753–787.

Long, Pamela O. (1997) 'Power, Patronage, and the Authorship of Ars: From Mechanical Know-How to Mechanical Knowledge in the Last Scribal Age', *Isis*, Vol. 88, No. 1 (Mar 1997), pp. 1–41.

Lorenz, Katharina and Jas Elsner, '"On the Relationship of Art History and Art Theory": Translators' Introduction', *Critical Inquiry*, Vol. 35, No. 1 (Autumn 2008), pp. 33–42.

Molland, A. G. (1968) 'The Geometrical Background to the "Merton School": An Exploration into the Application of Mathematics to Natural Philosophy in the Fourteenth Century', *The British Journal for the History of Science,* Vol. 4, No. 2 (Dec 1968), pp. 108–125.

Moxey, Keith (1995) 'Perspective, Panofsky, and the Philosophy of History', *New Literary History*, Vol. 26, No. 4, Philosophical Resonances (Autumn 1995), pp. 775–786.

Pedersen, Olaf (1993) *Early physics and astronomy: a historical introduction* (Rev. ed.), Cambridge University Press.

Podro, Michael (1982) *The Critical Historians of Art*, Yale University.

Rubenstein, Richard L. and John K. Roth (2003) *Approaches to Auschwitz: The Holocaust and Its Legacy*, Louisville, Kentucky: Westminster John Knox Press.

Schildgen, Brenda Deen (2009) 'Poetry and Theology in the Fourteenth Century', *Religion & Literature*, Vol. 41, No. 2 (Summer 2009), pp. 136–142.

Schubert, Hermann (1892) 'The Magic Square', *The Monist*, Vol. 2, No. 4 (July 1892), pp. 487–511.

Shin, Un-Chol (1990) 'Panofsky, Polanyi, and Intrinsic Meaning', *The Journal of Aesthetic Education*, Vol. 24, No. 4 (Winter 1990), pp. 17–32.

Sorensen, Lee. 'Wittkower, Rudolf', *Dictionary of Art Historians* Available at: www.dictionaryofarthistorians.org/wittkowerr.htm [Accessed 27 Nov. 2000].

Steinweis, Alan E. (1993) *Art, Ideology, and Economics in Nazi Germany: The Reich Chambers of Music, Theater, and the Visual Arts*, The University of North Carolina Press.

Van Maelsaeke, D. (1969) 'Dürer and Leonardo: A Comparative Study', *Theoria: A Journal of Social and Political Theory*, No. 33 (Oct 1969), pp. 45–62.

Van de Waal, H. (1972) *In Memoriam Erwin Panofsky, March 30, 1892 – March 14, 1968*, Amsterdam: Noord-Hollandsche U. M.

Wind, Edgar (1925) 'Theory of Art versus Aesthetics', *The Philosophical Review*, Vol. 34, No. 4 (July 1925), pp. 350–359.

Wölfflin, Heinrich (1915) Trs. M. D. Hottinger, *Principles of Art History, The Problem of the Development of Style in Later Art*, Seventh edn. 1950, Dover Publications Inc.

Zilsel, Edgar (1942) 'The Sociological Roots of Science', *Social Studies of Science*, Vol. 30, No. 6 (Dec 2000), pp. 935–949.

Biography

Alice Bowden is a writer and editor based in Suffolk, UK. Having worked in book publishing for 20 years, Alice went on to study an MA in Art History at the Open University. She then set up her own publishing company, Bowden & Brazil Ltd, writing the first book in this *Who the hell is...?* series. As well as running the day-to-day business of the company, Alice commissions and edits the other books in the series.

Acknowledgements

I would like to thank Thomas Bowden for the cover design and in particular for all his support, Sarah Tomley for her (always) excellent editing, Christopher Reid for his Latin translation of Panofsky's final poem in Chapter 1, Jan Fornachon for her German translations of Panofsky's book titles and Pam Asbury for her help with obtaining permissions. This is for T, M and T.

Picture Credits:

All illustrations by Hamael Khan. **Fig. 1** 'Erwin Panofsky (1892–1968)', courtesy of Alamy Ltd. **Fig. 2** 'Institute for Advanced Studies, Princeton, New Jersey, USA', Hanno Rein (https://commons.wikimedia.org/wiki/File:Institute_for_Advanced_Study_Campus.jpg), „Institute for Advanced Study Campus“, https://creativecommons.org/licenses/by-sa/3.0/legalcode **Fig. 3** 'A 19th-century magic lantern, as would have been used by Wölfflin' Andrei Niemimäki (https://commons.wikimedia.org/wiki/File:Magic_Lantern.jpg), „Magic Lantern“, https://creativecommons.org/licenses/by-sa/2.0/legalcode. Fig. 6 'Differing rules of perspective' courtesy of Zone Books in New York. **Fig. 7** 'Warburg Institute, formed in Hamburg, Germany, and later moved to London where it became affiliated with the University of London', Philafrenzy (https://commons.wikimedia.org/wiki/File:The_Warburg_Institute.JPG), https://creativecommons.org/licenses/by-sa/4.0/legalcode. **Fig. 13** 'Judith by Francesco Maffei, c. 1650–60, Pinacoteca Comunale de Faenza, Faenza, Italy'. Bigoldnance (https://commons.wikimedia.org/wiki/File:Maffei_Judith.jpg), https://creativecommons.org/licenses/by-sa/4.0/legalcode. **Fig.14 & 17** 'Melencolia I by Albrecht Dürer (1514)'. Albrecht Dürer artist QS:P170,Q5580 (https://commons.wikimedia.org/wiki/File:Melencolia_I_(Durero).jpg), „Melencolia I (Durero)“, marked as public domain, more details on Wikimedia Commons: https://commons.wikimedia.org/wiki/Template:PD-old. **Fig. 16** 'Typus Geometriae, Margarita Philosophica (1504 and 1508), Gregor Reisch'. Gregor Reisch (https://commons.wikimedia.org/wiki/File:Margarita_Philosophica_-_Typus_Geometriae.tif), „Margarita Philosophica - Typus Geometriae“, marked as public domain, more details on Wikimedia Commons: https://commons.wikimedia.org/wiki/Template:PD-old.

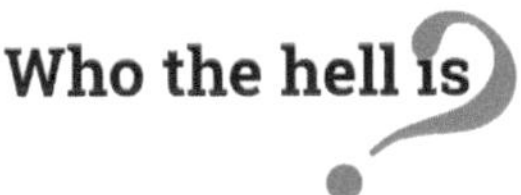

This exciting new series of books sets out to explore the life and theories of the world's leading intellectuals in a clear and understandable way. The series currently includes the following subject areas:

Art History | Psychology | Philosophy | Sociology | Politics

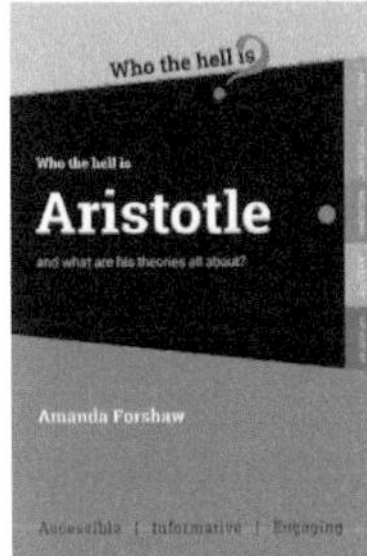

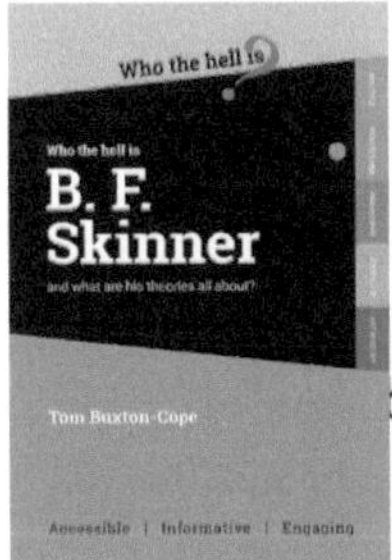

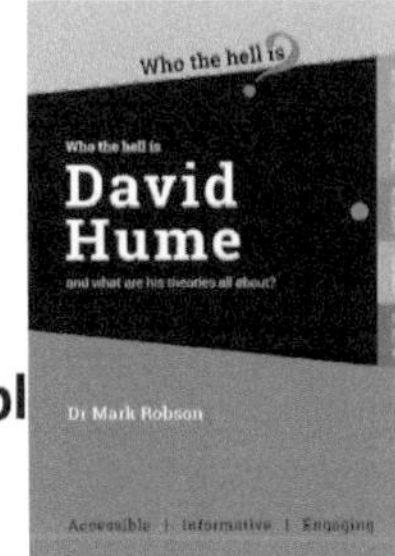

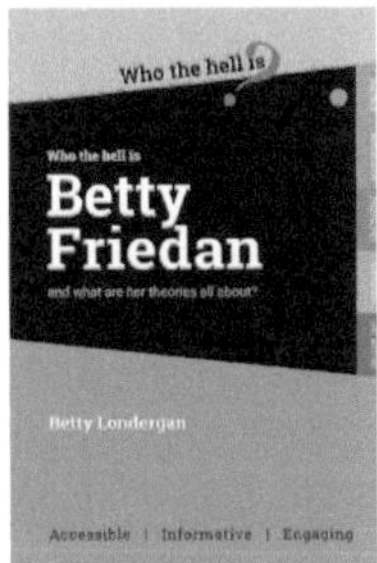

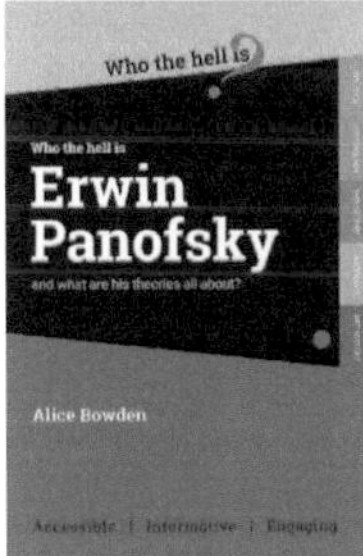

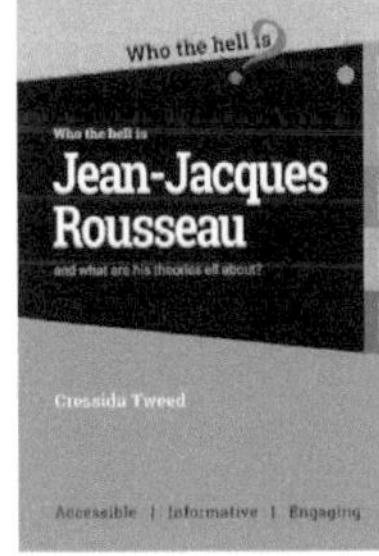

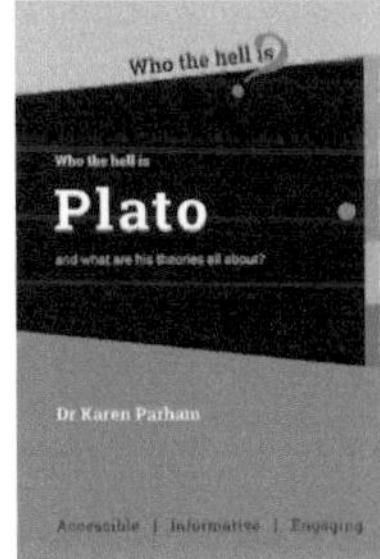

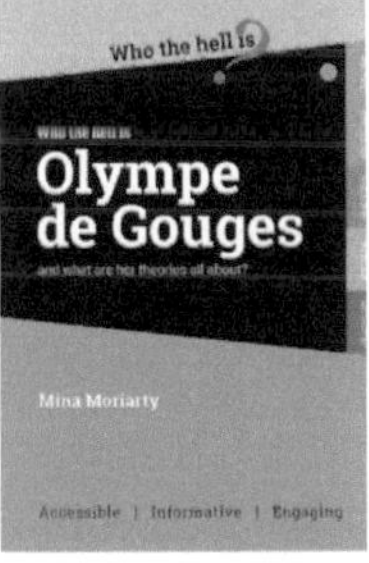

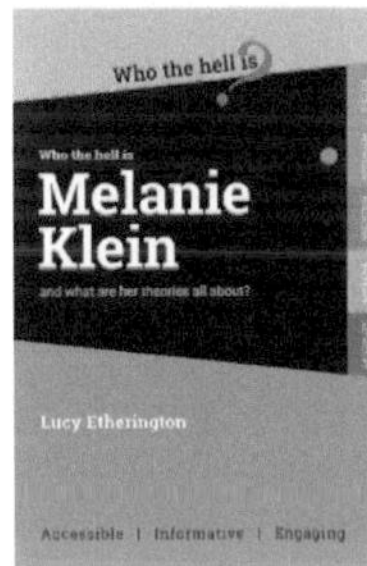

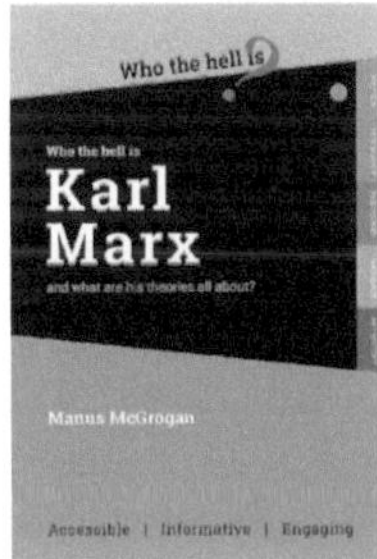

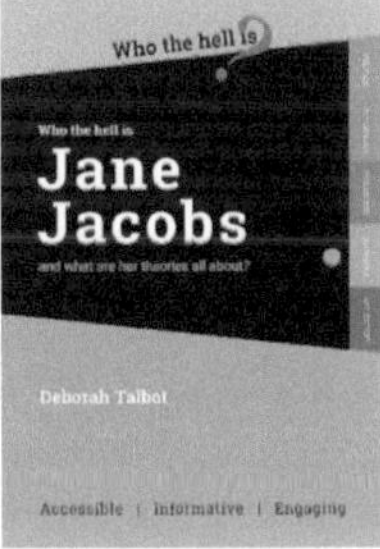

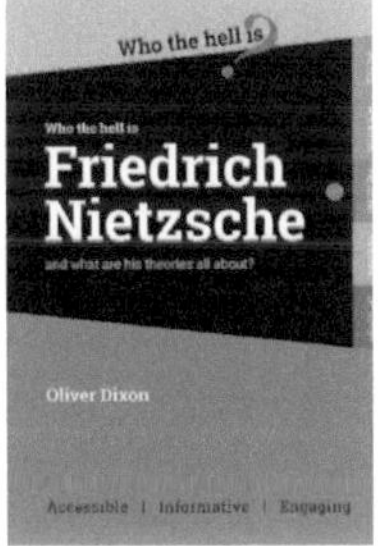

For more information about forthcoming titles in the Who the hell is...? series, go to: **www.whothehellis.co.uk**.

If any of our readers would like to put in a request for a particular intellectual to be included in our series, then please contact us at **info@whothehellis.co.uk**.

www.ingramcontent.com/pod-product-compliance
Ingram Content Group UK Ltd.
Pitfield, Milton Keynes, MK11 3LW, UK
UKHW041641190726
13854UKWH00006B/2632